# THAT'S MY SON

*How Moms Can Influence Boys to Become Men of Character*

RICK JOHNSON

Revell
Grand Rapids, Michigan

Published by Revell
a division of Baker Publishing Group
P.O. Box 6287, Grand Rapids, MI 49516-6287
www.revellbooks.com

Repackaged edition published 2017
ISBN 978-0-8007-2793-2

Printed in the United States of America



The Library of Congress has cataloged the previous edition as follows:
Johnson, Rick, 1956–
That's my son : how moms can influence boys to become men of character / Rick Johnson.
p. cm.
Includes bibliographical references.
ISBN 10: 0-8007-3077-1
ISBN 978-0-8007-3077-2
1. Mothers and sons—Religious aspects—Christianity. 2. Child rearing—Religious aspects—Christianity. 3. Sons—Religious life. I. Title.
BV4529.18.J648 2005
248.8′431—dc22 2004029415



17 18 19 20 21 22 23 7 6 5 4 3 2 1

# Contents


Acknowledgments 7
Introduction 9

1. Your Place in God's Plan for Your Son 13
2. Why Are Boys *So* Different? 23
3. Pitfalls—What to Avoid 45
4. Boys and Sex 65
5. Communicating with Boys 83
6. Disciplining Boys 101
7. What Do Boys Need to Learn to Become Good Men? 121
8. Respect 145
9. The Importance of Male Role Models 155
10. Where Do I Go from Here? 171

Resources 181
Notes 185

# Acknowledgments

I'd like to thank bold, courageous men such as Robert Lewis, Steve Farrar, Ken Canfield, Dennis Rainey, John Eldredge, and most of all, Stu Weber for teaching me what it is to be a man and a father. Stu, thanks for saving my life. I have borrowed heavily from the wisdom of these men and others in writing this book. Any mistakes are all mine and not due to the teachings of these modern-day knights. Thanks also to Michael Gurian for leading the way.

I'd also like to thank Joanne, Daina, Linda, Terry, Diane, Aimee, Renee, Bonnie, Diann, Julie, and Carrie for their input and encouragement. A big thanks also to Dr. Vicki Crumpton for her patience and encouragement while editing this book.

Most importantly, I owe a huge debt of gratitude to my wife, Suzanne, for her unending patience with me over the years as I grew from a little boy (at twenty-five years old) to, I hope at least, some semblance of a good man at the age of forty-eight. Without her unfailing faith, encouragement, and confidence while standing next to me, I could have accomplished nothing worthwhile in life.

# Introduction

You hear his little feet stomping up the wooden porch steps fast as they can go on a summer's afternoon. You yell, "Don't slam the screen d—" *SLAM!*

"Mom! Mom!" he hollers, so out of breath he can hardly get the words out. *Why are boys so loud?* you think. You hand him a glass of water, and he attempts to drink and tell his oh-so-important story at the same time.

"Mom—*GULP*—I—*GULP*—saw—*GULP, PANT, PANT*—the most—*GULP*— biggest—*GULP, PANT, PANT . . .*"

You smile at him and gently push the hair from his eyes, lovingly studying his countenance. What you see causes your heart to melt like the chocolate bar he left on your dashboard in the hot sun. His smudged face, his dirty T-shirt, and the grass-stained knees of his jeans tell you he's been on some outrageous adventure about which you can only guess. His hair is damp with sweat, and he's got that incredible boy smell about him—one part fresh-cut grass, one part odor of dog, one part unwashed hands that have been who knows where, and one part long-lost dreams from your own childhood. You gaze at him with love, wondering what he will be like as a man.

Then with a start you think, *How am I ever going to raise this little guy into a good man?*

What makes boys so special? Is it their love of bugs, dirt, dogs, baseball, explosions, loud noises, heavy equipment, and Kool-Aid? Or is it because they don't like taking baths, being kissed, eating vegetables, or having their noses wiped and ears cleaned? To mothers, these and all the other things that make boys special can present a confusing mix of contradictions. Particularly to women who were not raised with brothers or even a father, the odors, noises, and general rambunctiousness of boys can be downright frightening, or at the very least overwhelming.

I count myself fortunate to operate a nonprofit organization called Better Dads. Better Dads is a fathering skills training program with the goal of inspiring and equipping men to be more involved in their children's lives. Through workshops and small group settings, we help men become better fathers.

Several years ago Kevin, a counselor at a local school district, approached me and said that his elementary schools had a number of single mothers with questions about raising boys. He asked if I could address their needs through a seminar, and that is how my seminar, *Courageous Moms: Raising Boys to Become Good Men*, was born. The key word is *good*. Your son will become a man regardless of what you do or don't do. But your goal should be to raise a good man. And that, I think, takes some special training and skills that are becoming rare in today's culture.

While putting together the single moms seminar, I talked with a number of single mothers who had successfully raised boys to become good men. I ran my ideas by them for approval and incorporated their most successful techniques into the program. Since then, I have given numerous presentations to groups of single moms and have never failed to be touched by their earnest desire for information on how to raise their sons to be good men. I've discovered that there's much value to the old adage "It's easier to raise a boy than to fix a man."

After I started presenting the seminars, I discovered a very interesting phenomenon. Women in general, not just single moms, were very interested in learning how boys (and men) think, act, and feel and why they think, act, and feel the way they do. Married women and even those who were not yet mothers began attending the seminars.

Even though I'm a fathering advocate, I have nothing but respect and admiration for mothers, especially single mothers, who are interested in trying to help grow their sons to become good men. The horrifying truth is that 85 percent of custodial single parents are mothers. I can't begin to fathom how difficult it must be to raise and provide for a family without the support of a spouse.

It's important for you to understand that I'm not a psychiatrist, a psychologist, or even a trained counselor. I'm also not an expert father, to which my kids will readily attest. I make mistakes every day. I'm just an average parent like most of you, trying to raise my kids the best I can. I've just been fortunate to have received some extra training and to have read many good books.

Also, it's important to understand that I will be using some generalizations throughout this book. These are meant to portray characteristics men and women can relate to, not to promote stereotypes.

One thing I'm not going to tell you is how to be a mother. You're a better mother than I'll ever be. But maybe I can provide some insight into what it takes to be a man. After all, I am a man—by some accounts, a fairly good man—I've been a boy, and I've raised a pretty good son nearly into manhood. I've worked with hundreds of men over the years, learning about their childhoods and the areas they struggle with daily. That doesn't make me an expert, but hopefully, it will allow me to give you some insight into what makes us males tick.

Having said that, I dedicate this book to all the moms out there who are struggling to make it. Moms who work all day and come home and cook meals and clean the house, sometimes with little or no support from the father of their children. Moms who do without day after day so their kids can eat, have a roof over their heads, and have shoes and clothes to wear. Moms who are trying their best to raise a family on their own without the resources and support of a two-parent family. Moms who, despite the hardships, never quit.

I hope this book will ease your burden by helping you understand how boys think, how best to communicate with these strange little creatures, and how to help them become *good* men so that someday your grandchildren will look up at you and say, "Thank you, Grandma, for raising such a good daddy for me."

# I

# Your Place in God's Plan for Your Son

With sympathy and with reverence we greet you on the soil ennobled by the blood of your courageous sons, whose sacrifices have created a bond between us which can never be broken. The world cannot measure your tragic loss. You have suffered in silence and alone with courage and love. You have given to the Great Cause something more precious than your own life blood. And the altar of freedom is wet with your tears.

*French general, speech to the American mothers who voyaged to France to visit the graves of their dead sons*

In 480 BC, Greece was the hub of Western civilization. Ancient Greece was divided into separate provinces or city-states that warred among themselves. The greatest of these city-states was Sparta. The Spartans were a warlike people who trained young men from birth in the art of war. They used strenuous techniques to train boys in self-discipline, courage, teamwork, and warfare. It was a way of life for them. Their women eschewed makeup and the frilly coverings common to other Grecian women and participated in athletic competitions, even training as warriors. Nevertheless, Spartan women were admired throughout Greece for their grace and natural beauty.

To the east, the Persian king Xerxes (whose father had lost an earlier war to Greece) had amassed an army of over three hundred thousand men. Xerxes' plan was to conquer Greece and complete his goal of worldwide domination while avenging his father's defeat. The Greeks realized they had to mobilize themselves in order to save their homeland.

The huge Persian army would be landing in eastern Greece, which provided the shortest and least dangerous crossing of the Aegean Sea. The Greeks' only chance was to stall the Persians long enough to mobilize the Greek army and quickly build up their naval fleet to arrive and engage the larger Persian navy that would be used to supply the invasion.

The Spartans stepped forward and volunteered to stall the Persian army at a narrow valley called Thermopylae, or the Hot Gates. Thermopylae was a small opening through the mountains, about sixty men wide, abutted by high, steep cliffs on both sides and the ocean at one end. The Spartan king Leonidas chose three hundred men (including himself) to defend the pass against the Persian onslaught. These three hundred men, along with several thousand allies from other provinces, held the huge Persian army at bay for six days, killing a great number of the invading army.

Finally, a Greek traitor went to Xerxes and told him of a goat path through the mountains that would allow the Persians to get behind the Spartans. Xerxes sent ten thousand of his Immortals (royal guards) across the mountains. When Leonidas found out he had been betrayed, he sent the allied forces home to defend their homes and cities. Leonidas and the remainder of the three hundred Spartans made a last stand in a circle upon a hillside. They were slain to the last man, but they delayed the Persian army long enough for their allies to escape safely.

The Spartans' bravery allowed the Greek army time to mobilize and the Greek fleet time to arrive and engage the Persian navy. Their heroism inspired the Greeks to victory over the much larger invading force.

So what does that story have to do with you as the mother of a son?

Shortly before the battle at Thermopylae, Leonidas was secretly asked how he had chosen the three hundred brave men for the suicide mission to defend the Hot Gates. After all, the men appeared to be an eclectic mix of odd choices—grizzled veterans of many campaigns alongside young men unbloodied in battle. To die for your city was the greatest privilege a Spartan could achieve, and all warriors wanted the honor. Did he pick the bravest men, the best fighters, the greatest Olympic athletes? Or did he choose the fastest, strongest, and wisest men he could find?

Leonidas stated that none of those traits factored into how he chose the three hundred. Instead, he chose them based on the character of their wives and mothers. He reasoned that Thermopylae would not be the deciding battle of the war—that would come later on the plains of Greece. Since all the men at Thermopylae were destined to be killed, their wives and mothers would be left for the rest of Greece to see. If these women were broken by the loss of their husbands and sons, then the Greeks would lose heart and fail to defend their homeland. But if these women exhibited courage and strength, then the Grecian peoples would be inspired and win the war. Leonidas said, "These brave women are to be the new Mothers of Greece. All of the people will be inspired by their dry-eyed example of courage and sacrifice."[1] Apparently, these extraordinary women performed up to his expectations.

The Spartan moms saw the bigger picture and were willing to sacrifice their own feelings and loved ones for the well-being of their nation. They raised up sons who would fulfill the destiny of their times and would be remembered twenty-five hundred years later. Each of us, men and women, has a destiny from God to fulfill. In the greatest maternal sacrifice in history, Mary had to watch the gruesome torture and crucifixion of her son Jesus as part of God's plan for the eternal salvation of humankind. Part of your calling is to raise up your son to fulfill God's plan for him.

The Bible urges, "Train up a child in the way he should go, and when he is old he will not depart from it" (Prov. 22:6). *Train up* means "to dedicate," which includes stimulating the child to do good through guidance, discipline, and encouragement. A parent's main task is to receive a child as a charge from the Lord and then to dedicate the child to God's ways.

Numerous examples are given throughout the Bible of women who inspired their sons to be the men God wanted them to be. The Bible urges you to do this boldly and courageously without intimidation. Training up your boys to be bold will require you to be bold and courageous as well.

As a mother, you hold the fate of the world in your hands. Men are currently abdicating their roles as leaders in their homes, their communities, and their country in record numbers. This is creating a crisis that is threatening to dissolve the very fabric of society, destroying our country and possibly even the world. Men in our country are mired in apathy and passivity. The reason? They are not being brought up to relish their God-given role as protector of and provider for their families.

Men who do relish this role stand in the gap between a life filled with God's blessings and the total moral decay and collapse of our civilization.

As a mother, you have the ability, even the responsibility, to ensure that your son is raised up to be a man who will lead with courage and integrity. That's a huge responsibility but one that women have been charged with since the beginning of time.

Mothers have sacrificed their sons, both literally and figuratively, for the greater good of society throughout history. As a mother, do you think you're not important? Think again. The power of a mother's influence is like a steady river carving canyons through the landscape of history. The legacy you leave as the teacher and nurturer of the next generation of men is valuable beyond description. The Spartan moms' story is just one example that shows the importance of mothers in the lives of men and in shaping the history of civilization.

## God's Plan for Your Son

> A house means a family house, a place specially meant for putting children and men in so as to restrict their waywardness and distract them from the longing for adventure and escape they've had since time began.
>
> Marguerite Duras, *Practicalities*

We were created for the incredible adventure of changing the world through Jesus Christ. We intuitively know it; we just don't always consciously understand it. All of us long for significance in our very souls, for something greater than individual success, material goods, sexual conquests, and even power.

Don't believe me? Then why are so many famous people unhappy even though they are talented, rich, and powerful? We hear every day about famous people battling with drug and alcohol addictions, marital troubles, and sexual infidelity. What's going on? Don't fame and fortune provide us with all the happiness we require? Why do we continue to struggle and want more and more even after achieving what the world considers success? Call it thirst and hunger for the truth—for significance in our lives. We all long for significance, especially men. That's why boys have big dreams of adventures and heroic deeds.

John Eldredge in *Wild at Heart* talks about the fact that every man needs a journey to take, a dragon to slay, and a damsel to rescue. He contends that most men in our country are "soft men." They're passive, indecisive, and apathetic. Our culture and even the church have feminized men to the point where our greatest ambition is just to be a "nice guy."[2]

Is this true? Has society softened men? I believe it has. Why? Because unfortunately, men today seem more moved by their emotions or by cultural mores than by their principles. We don't want to be labeled as intolerant or judgmental, or even be ostracized as politically incorrect. We fold under the scrutiny of public opinion—of whatever the television and newspaper tell us. Couple that with the lack of positive male role models in many homes and it's no wonder boys don't grow up knowing how to act like men.

Most men think they're simply here on earth to kill time, and frankly, it's killing them. Men are angry and don't even know why.[3] Henry David Thoreau said, "Most men live lives of quiet desperation." I sense that desperation in many of the men I meet.

Eldredge maintains that men tend to pick only the battles they're sure to win, attempt only those adventures they can handle, and pursue only those women they're sure to conquer.[4] I remember as a young man being secretly entranced by a beautiful young lady, but she was too beautiful and too popular, so I never even tried to risk chasing after her. I thought, *There is no way she would ever be interested in someone like me*. However, God wants us to stretch and reach for the impossible—to take risks. Our faith, submission to him, and willingness to be used by him enable us to achieve greatness in his name.

I realize as I look back on most of my life that my decisions and choices were governed by a fear of failure. I never risked doing anything great for fear of failure or loss of face. Mel Gibson, as William Wallace, said in the movie *Braveheart,* "All men die; not every man really lives." I don't believe you can ever really live if you don't risk failure by attempting to do great things. That's what makes life worth living, and God blesses a man's honorable endeavors.

God created men to be passionate and fierce and noble. We have a spiritual longing for adventure, for a battle to fight that's bigger than ourselves, for significance in our lives.[5] We can feel that longing in our souls. Something is missing from our lives. We men long to be dangerous, to do things that make us and others uncomfortable, to tackle insurmountable odds, and to change the world. That attitude scares a passive world. That's why they want to soften us. Our culture considers Christian men who are not passive or complacent to be dangerous. But that is exactly how God wants men to be known.

We need women to be Spartan mothers. To raise up spiritual warriors who will go out and fulfill God's destiny for them of changing the world—to make a difference, to be significant. To inflame the passions God put in your boy so that he might fulfill his destiny as a man. The fact that men are abandoning their families in droves is destroying our country. I'm convinced that fatherlessness is directly or indirectly the cause of nearly every problem we face as a society today. We must stop this plague before our culture disappears like ancient Greece. I work with many men in an attempt to change this trend, but I believe it may be too late to reverse this epidemic in our generation. The only way to stop it is to raise up the current generation of boys to be brave-hearted stalwarts of virtue and character.

Our world desperately needs Spartan moms at a time such as this. This book will help you meet the challenge of raising your son to be a *good* man. It will give you direction to steer your son to become a man of character, a man who lives a life of significance, creating a better world in which to live. A man of destiny, loving and encouraging his wife as Jesus loves the church and raising his children with the calming wisdom and grace of our heavenly Father.

This book will challenge you and may even make you angry from time to time. That does not make the wisdom in it any less true. My hope is that you learn as much and have as much fun reading this book as I did writing it.

I wish you all God's blessings on the incredible journey you're about to undertake.

## Questions for Discussion

1. Are you prepared to be a Spartan mom? Would you be willing to sacrifice your son (literally or figuratively) to a cause greater than himself? If not, what do you think is holding you back?
2. Do you agree with the author's assertion that we were created for the incredible adventure of changing the world through Christ? Why or why not?
3. Discuss with another woman or with your group how men's character can be a factor either for creating a better world for women and children or for leaving a legacy of hopelessness.

# 2

# Why Are Boys *So* Different?

> So God created man in His own image; in the image of God He created him; male and female He created them.
>
> *Genesis 1:27*

> And the LORD God caused a deep sleep to fall on Adam, and he slept; and He took one of his ribs, and closed up the flesh in its place. Then the rib which the LORD God had taken from man He made into a woman.
>
> *Genesis 2:21–22*

Let's look at some of the things that make men and women different from one another. While researching the differences between the sexes for this chapter, I decided to check the Internet. I entered "differences between males and females" on the Google search engine and promptly received hits for 1,360,000 websites. The websites covered anatomical, psychological, sexual, genetic, and verbal differences and everything imaginable in between.

God created both sexes—male and female—equal yet different from one another. Differences do not indicate that one sex is superior or inferior to the other. Each sex was created with different strengths and weaknesses so that together we equal a whole greater than the sum of its parts.

## Physiology

That being said, one of the ways males differ from females is physiologically. Researchers have recently begun using computerized axial tomography (CAT), magnetic resonance imaging (MRI), and other brain-scan equipment to measure how male and female brains respond to various kinds of stimulation. They've discovered that while a male's brain is slightly larger, a female's brain has a larger corpus callosum—the bundle of nerves that connects the left and right hemispheres of the brain. This allows females to use more of each hemisphere of the brain, allowing more communication between the two sides of the brain. Male brains primarily use one hemisphere of the brain at a time. The consequences of these differences will be more apparent when we discuss communication and multitasking skills later on in this book. This developmental difference explains why females tend to be better readers than males and why males have a harder time identifying an emotion they see on someone else's face. This may also help explain why many women feel that the men in their lives don't understand their emotions well and why women are generally more intuitive than men.[1]

When we were first married, I used to disparage my wife's "womanly intuition." However, over the years I've become mature enough to notice that Suzanne's observations, particularly about other people, are nearly always accurate. For example, sometimes we'll meet people and she will have a bad feeling about them. I used to ignore her warnings or pass them off as foolishness, and then we would later discover that a person did in fact have some significant character flaws I had been unable to deduce at the time.

While I typically use logic, Suzanne is much more adept at reading other people's mannerisms, posture, and emotions—detecting their thoughts and feelings and hidden character flaws (though she's not likely to be able to explain it to my satisfaction). Now we use her intuitive skills as a useful tool in our decision-making process. I don't even question her intuition. I just take her gut-level feelings at face value. If she says she has a bad feeling about someone, even if she can't explain why, I accept it as truth.

## Hormones

Males are hardwired to be more aggressive than females. This is primarily due to the hormone testosterone, which is responsible for maleness. Males typically have up to twenty times more testosterone than females, causing more dominant and aggressive behavior. This hormone also promotes muscle growth and body hair. Consequently, males are generally bigger, faster, and stronger (and hairier) and have larger upper body mass than females.

Due to higher levels of testosterone, males tend to act out in times of stress. Females tend to become withdrawn in similar circumstances. In stressful situations (during their parents' divorce, for instance), adolescent males often become angry and aggressive, getting into trouble and acting out, whereas adolescent females are more prone to become depressed and withdrawn.

Michael Gurian, in his excellent book *A Fine Young Man*, sums up adolescent boys this way:

> They tread carefully on some things and seem to push forward like maniacs in others. A fire inside them motivates them and then seems to go out suddenly, leaving them exhausted and able to sleep until noon. They both crave structure and despise it, sometimes leaving their parents, mentors, and educators breathless. They seem to save up all their words only for television shows or ideas or activities *they* care about. They seem to need their friends now more than their families. They even stink a little bit. Is it the constantly dirty socks, or is it the testosterone-induced body odor that they now wear like a badge?[2]

I can tell you from personal experience how this hormone affects a man. Several years ago my body stopped producing enough testosterone. For about six months, until we discovered the problem, I felt lethargic, passive, weak, indecisive, and timid; had a low libido; and just generally felt miserable. I was missing something intangible—call it my "mojo" or my maleness. The whole experience left me feeling sort of like Superman when he's exposed to kryptonite. However, immediately upon fixing the problem—Boom! I had my strength, decision-making ability, and ambition back. I felt alive and active, with a renewed sex drive. I felt like a man again.

The chromosomes a baby receives from its father and mother determine its sexual identity. If the embryo receives a Y chromosome from its father's DNA, it is flooded with a "testosterone wash" during the sixth week of gestation. This testosterone bath changes the structure of the brain as well as the way the two hemispheres relate to each other.

The other time period in which testosterone plays a big role in the development of boys is puberty. During puberty testosterone deluges the body of the male child, causing his genitalia to increase eight times in size. In their book *Raising Sons and Loving It!* Gary and Carrie Oliver write,

> During this testosterone wash the level of testosterone is ten to twenty times stronger in boys than girls. The prepubertal and adolescent boy will have between five to seven surges of testosterone per day—an increase marked by a tendency to masturbate frequently, be moody and aggressive, want more sleep, lose his temper more often, be negative and critical, act like his head is in the clouds, and have a significantly greater interest in sex.[3]

Another hormone that influences gender behavior is serotonin, also a neurotransmitter. Its purpose is to pacify and soothe emotions—to control impulsive behavior. It's no surprise, then, that females produce more of this hormone than males. In addition, postpubescent males seem to process this hormone more readily, which may explain why they suffer from depression much less than females.

A third physiological factor affecting boys' behavior is a small gland called the amygdala. The amygdala is a walnut-size portion of the brain that acts as an emotional computer. In times of perceived threat or danger, it orders the adrenal glands and other defensive organs into action. The amygdala is larger in males than in females, thus explaining why males tend to be more aggressive.[4]

## Psychology

Males differ markedly from females psychologically as well. Males are typically better at math, science, spatial relations, logic, and reasoning than females. Females have better language skills, make fewer mistakes, take fewer risks, and are better students than males. They are typically more compassionate to others, more intuitive, and less impulsive than their male counterparts.

Brain-scanning equipment has not only pointed out developmental and biochemical differences between males and females, but it has also been used to study structural differences. Studies at the University of Pennsylvania have determined how different parts of the brain are activated depending on the task the brain is engaged in.

Subjects were asked to do a spatial task such as figuring out how two parts to a puzzle fit together. Results showed that in most of the males, the right hemisphere lit up intensely, while the left hemisphere lit up less brightly. In the female brain, both hemispheres lit up equally but less intensely than the males' right hemispheres. Researchers concluded that, on the average, males do better at spatial tasks than females—presumably because they can draw heavily on the right hemisphere of the brain to solve problems.

Additionally, during verbal tests, males used much less of their brains than females did. Research indicates that the female brain is activated continuously during verbal tasks, while the male brain switches on and off.[5]

Having coached girls' and boys' basketball for a number of years, I've observed some significant differences in the way each sex plays the game. Girls just do not grasp the spatial relation concepts involved in the game as well as boys. The spacing on the court and the angles required to both score and defend against the opposing player are much harder to teach to girls—even at the high school level.

For example, when a full-court pass is thrown, defenders must simultaneously judge the speed of the ball, the speed of the player, the angle of the ball, and the spot on the floor in which all three come together. Add to that calculation the fact that they must determine their own speed and the angle they must take to arrive at that spot at the appropriate time. The girls who do grasp these concepts exhibit much better "court sense" and are far and away better players than those who don't. Boys intuitively understand these concepts at a young age. Additionally, trying to teach girls to be aggressive on the court can be difficult. For most—not all, but most—it seems to go against their nature.

However, girls do seem to understand the concept of teamwork much better than boys do and frequently develop stronger bonds during the course of a season. I also believe girls are much more coachable, taking direction better than boys and coming together as a team sooner.

After having coached boys' basketball, I took over a sixth-grade girls' team. During one of the first practices, I yelled at one of the girls as I would have at a boy. Boys rarely get upset by being yelled at—in fact, it works well to motivate them. This time, the young lady in question burst into tears and ran off to the restroom. The rest of the team stopped practicing, looked at me with disdain, and bolted after the girl to console her. They looked like a herd of antelope, moving together in perfect symmetry. Afterward, my daughter proceeded to read me the riot act, telling me why the girl was so sensitive at this particular time. After receiving much more personal information than I needed or was comfortable with, I immediately revised the way I communicated with the team.

Another example of gender differences occurred later that same year when a player on the opposing team fell down during a game. Immediately the game stopped, and half of my team went over to help her up. I've even seen this scenario happen in girls' high school games! After going nearly apoplectic the first few times I witnessed this event, I've learned to take this kind of gamesmanship in stride. Take my word for it: you will seldom see boys at any age lose the advantage during competition to help an opposing player get up off the floor.

Males are typically much more competitive than females. Competition is a big part of a male's life and typically colors his view of every circumstance and relationship at least to some degree. Ever wonder why men can't stand to have someone pass them on the freeway or why men are reluctant to ask for directions? To boys, competition is part of the game. It feels good to have boundaries established and to know where you stand in the pecking order. That's why rules and regulations are important to males—it gives them a framework by which to judge themselves and others. Without rules there is no order, and chaos quickly ensues.

Because of the way their minds process information, boys prefer to view objects that move quickly. Hence, they are more at risk to become addicted to television, video games, and the Internet. Nearly all video games are marketed to boys. Even the way males and females navigate tells a story—women personalize space by finding landmarks; men see a geometric system, taking directional cues in the layout of routes.

Boys (and, I'm embarrassed to admit, men as well) take in less sensory data and have a shorter attention span than females. I can thoroughly rifle through a drawer or cupboard and not find what I'm searching for, no matter how hard I look. Yet my wife can walk right up and find that item instantly. This is not an occasional occurrence. I have to scratch my head in wonder, because my wife accuses me of not really looking, yet I know I've searched to the best of my ability. I hear repeatedly from other women who confirm that their boys and men suffer from the same affliction.

## Characteristics Common to Boys

At the risk of promoting stereotypes, there are certain characteristics that seem to distinguish boys from girls.

Boys play more aggressively, climbing everything in sight, all the while hitting, running, and jumping at every opportunity. Girls are more likely to play corporately, with the goal of building relationships. Females live longer than males and typically perform better in certain stressful environments. Females also suffer more from depression than males. Boys are more prone to be hyperactive, are more nonverbal, become later readers, are more aggressive, are bigger risk takers, and are more adventurous. Males more often operate in a detached and isolated fashion. Solitary work to master a skill is a common characteristic of male life, and men are quicker to dismiss the claims of other people and even their own emotions. This approach tends to make things (machines, ideas) at least as important as people in the man's inner life.[6] Compared to girls, boys

- are six times more likely to have learning disorders
- are three times more likely to be drug addicts
- are four times more likely to be diagnosed as emotionally disturbed
- are twelve times more likely to commit murder
- have a 50 percent greater risk of dying in a car accident
- are five times more likely to commit suicide

Boys comprise 90 percent of those in drug treatment programs, and 95 percent of the kids involved in juvenile court are boys.[7]

Besides suffering the consequences of their behavior, boys suffer significant physical and psychological problems as well. In *Raising Sons and Loving It!* the following differences are noted between boys and girls:

- Young boys are admitted to mental hospitals and juvenile institutions about seven times more frequently than girls of similar age and socioeconomic background.
- Boys are twice as likely as girls to suffer from autism and six times as likely to be diagnosed as having hyperkinesis, or attention deficit/hyperactivity disorder (ADHD).
- Boys stutter more and have significantly more learning and speech disabilities than girls. Some research suggests that dyslexia is found in up to nine times as many boys as girls.
- Boys are much more likely to suffer from a variety of birth defects.
- Boys are prone to schizophrenia and suffer a higher incidence of mental retardation. In fact, about two hundred genetic diseases affect only boys, including the most severe forms of muscular dystrophy and hemophilia.[8]

Boys enjoy outdoor play and games that include bodily contact and have a clearly defined winner and loser. This is how boys socialize and bond with each other. Often this type of behavior is mistaken for aggression. However, it's important that we do not mistake this rough-and-tumble behavior for unhealthy aggression. Unhealthy aggression, or violence, is destructive and shouldn't be allowed.

Healthy male aggressive behavior can be observed in sports. Contact sports like football, basketball, and wrestling provide positive outlets for healthy male aggression. In these competitions everyone starts out on the same level, and within the rules and framework of the game (which everyone is subject to), an individual's and the team's efforts make the difference between winning and losing. This allows a male to test himself against his peers and against himself. This helps create and build a positive self-image.

Unhealthy male aggression might take the form of bullying smaller peers or younger siblings. Aggression becomes violence when it violates another's core self. For instance, extreme acts of unhealthy male aggression occur in gang initiations, which often include ritualistic beatings for males or gang rape for females. Additionally, the win-at-all-costs mentality exhibited by some athletes and coaches promotes unhealthy aggression and violence.

If your son takes pleasure in picking on those weaker than himself, abuses animals, engages in continual fighting, or shows other signs of violent tendencies, consider seeking professional guidance to help him understand the difference between healthy and unhealthy aggression.

Fighting often serves as an outlet for unhealthy male aggression. Movies such as *Fight Club* underscore the search for an outlet for natural male aggression (albeit in an unhealthy manner) in our society, which frowns on many of the traditional male activities used for this purpose. For example, boyish games such as cops and robbers, cowboys and Indians, or war games are now widely considered politically incorrect, and the typically male pursuits of hunting and fishing are often viewed as boorish or even unacceptable.

But many authority figures in charge of boys, such as parents, teachers, and administrators, blur the lines of distinction between healthy and unhealthy aggression. Many educators today view the normal play of boys with disapproval or ban it outright.[9]

Christina Hoff Sommers, in her book *The War Against Boys,* reports that one Boston-area teacher, Barbara Wilder-Smith, spent a year observing elementary school classrooms. She reports that more and more "mothers and female teachers . . . believe that the key to producing a nonviolent adult is to remove all conflict—toy weapons, wrestling, shoving, and imaginary explosions and crashes—from a boy's life." She sees a growing chasm between the "culture of women and the culture of boys."[10]

Most of you who have children of each gender already know that boys and girls are different. They act differently, play differently, and talk differently.

Until recently, certain elements of society maintained that there were no differences between males and females except in their reproductive organs. The cultural movement over the past several decades, promoted primarily by the feminist movement and other "enlightened" intellectuals, exhorted parents to raise nonsexist, gender-neutral children. Advocates of this movement urged boys to play with dolls and explore their feminine side by engaging in games such as "house." Girls were not to be typecast with such games but were to be given the opportunity to participate in nonstereotypical gender bias activities. The folly of this theory was that, despite the parents' best efforts at directing the kids to play in cross-gender activities, the boys typically took the dolls and made guns out of them or threw them as hand grenades while playing war with each other, and the girls migrated together to play in more social activities such as tea parties.[11]

Unfortunately, the air of disruptiveness that surrounds boys can lead to diagnosis of problems where none exist. Especially for women not raised with brothers or a father, boys can seem like a shocking mix of smells, sounds, and noise. I have a friend who proposes that men don't mature much beyond the age of thirteen years or so. He may be right. When we all get together with our sons to go hunting or camping, the same loud, rude noises that set off our sons into gales of laughter still crack us up as well. Much of the charm of men may be the little boys they retain inside themselves.

## War on Boys

Perhaps because of males' disruptive nature, our culture has been on a crash course to feminize boys, or at least to soften them, for the past twenty years or so.

John Eldredge, author of *Wild at Heart*, says it like this: "The idea, widely held in our culture, is that the aggressive nature of boys is inherently bad, and we have to make them into something more like girls."[12]

Some schools have recently experimented with doing away with recess. Eliminating recess at school really hurts boys who have a difficult time staying still and concentrating for long periods of time. Without a physical outlet like recess to release their pent-up energy, they tend to exhibit distracting characteristics in the classroom. Far more boys are labeled with ADHD than girls. The fact that girls tend to be quieter, better behaved, and frankly, nicer in school than boys contributes to this imbalance. I'm not convinced that medicating a large percent of our young male population is a positive solution. Interestingly, several anecdotal stories have illustrated that introducing fathers or male father figures into the classroom on a volunteer basis has a calming influence on boys.

Take, for example, this story about elephants on a game preserve in Africa. Due to game management practices over the years, a herd of teenage bull elephants were left to fend for themselves. All of the older bulls had been culled from the herd, and the matriarchal leaders refused to allow the nearly grown "boy" elephants to mix with the cows and their young babies. This herd of young bulls was very aggressive, wreaking havoc on the countryside and neighboring villages. They were destroying crops and knocking down dwellings, as well as attacking the human population.

All the experts on elephants were called together for a conference to decide how to remedy this problem. After much fruitless discussion, they finally called in an old African chief, who told them, "Bring in an old bull." They located an old bull elephant in another part of the country, airlifted him in, and gently lowered him into the area where the herd had last been seen. The herd was not seen again for several more weeks, but one day there came the herd. Out from the dense forest came all of the young bulls, walking peacefully in a straight line behind the old bull, each minding his manners. No troubles were ever caused by the members of the herd again. The moral of this story is that males need the wise and mature leadership of older males. It directly affects their behavior.

Another example: About four years ago, I began playing basketball in a Christian men's recreational basketball league. I was far and away the oldest man playing, with most of the other members in their mid- to late twenties. One day I was talking to Chris, the executive director of the league.

"Chris, I just wanted to thank you for letting me play basketball. I know my skills and athletic ability are not what they once were."

Chris said, "That's okay. We like having you play. You provide a calming influence on the game."

At first I wasn't quite sure that was a compliment. However, after further discussion, Chris explained that as competitively as men play, the influence of an older male who conducts himself with self-control keeps the young guys from losing their tempers as often as they might without that influence.

The point is that neither the old bull elephant in the first story, nor I in the second story, led the younger males under our sphere of influence to change their behavior through physical size or strength. Neither of us was bigger or stronger than the younger males. We led them by modeling positive behavior. Younger males are always looking to older males to know how to act in certain situations, whether in school or life.

Christina Hoff Sommers says, "It's a bad time to be a boy in America. As the new millennium begins, the triumphant victory of our women's soccer team has come to symbolize the spirit of American girls. The defining event for boys is the shooting at Columbine High."[13] She goes on to say that the media and the feminists have portrayed boys to be the bane of society and the cause of most of its ills.

The premise, then, put forth by many special interest groups is that we must eradicate natural masculine behavior in young boys through social engineering programs in the public schools.

The war cry of these groups in the past has been that boys were given preferential treatment in schools much to the detriment of girls. This was epitomized a dozen years ago when Wellesley College researcher Susan Bailey wrote a report that made national headlines. Titled "How Schools Shortchange Girls," the study chronicled how teachers paid more attention to boys, steered girls away from math and science, and made schools more inviting to boys than to girls. However, a review of the facts today shows that boys are on the weak end of the educational gender gap. Boys are up to a year and a half behind girls in school and are less likely to attend college. In 1997 college enrollments consisted of 45 percent male and 55 percent female students. According to the U.S. Department of Education, this trend of declining male college enrollment will continue to worsen in the future.[14]

As I was writing this section, the *Oregonian* newspaper reported that 71 percent of the Portland/Vancouver high school valedictorians were female this past year. The article went on to say, "'It took less than 30 years for longstanding male dominance in college to be reversed, lightning speed for social change of that magnitude,' says Cornelius Riordan, professor of sociology at Providence College, who has tracked gender differences in education for years. 'In the early 1970s, 60 percent of college students were male. Now, roughly 60 percent of college students are female,' he says."[15]

While the behavior boys naturally exhibit needs to be controlled, we should remember that God created them this way. God's creation has accomplished some remarkable things in our world. Hoff Sommers summarizes by saying,

> This book [*The War Against Boys*] tells the story of how it has become fashionable to attribute pathology to millions of healthy male children. It is a story of how we are turning against boys and forgetting a simple truth: that the energy, competitiveness, and corporal daring of normal, decent males is responsible for much of what is right in the world. No one denies that boys' aggressive tendencies must be checked and channeled in constructive ways. Boys need discipline, respect, and moral guidance. Boys need love and tolerant understanding. They do not need to be pathologized.[16]

Or as the dissident feminist writer Camille Paglia puts it, "Masculinity is aggressive, unstable, combustible. It is also the most creative cultural force in history."[17]

Stress and pressure also affect the way boys behave. Kids today, especially teenagers, are exposed to a whole different set of problems and stresses than you or I experienced. Teenagers today have freedoms previously reserved for adults. The levels of violence, sex, and lack of respect for authority young people are exposed to daily on television and in the movies are beyond belief.

| Most Common High School Problems in the 1940s | Most Common High School Problems in the 1980s[18] |
|---|---|
| talking | drug abuse |
| chewing gum | alcohol abuse |
| making noise | pregnancy |
| running in halls | suicide |
| cutting in line | rape |
| dress code | robbery |
| littering | assault |

As the Olivers so aptly state in *Raising Sons and Loving It!* "Times have changed, priorities have changed, and values have changed—and few of these changes have been good for marriages, for families, or for our sons."[19]

Being a teenager has always been difficult, but today's youth are faced with consequences for their behavior that can lead to lifelong wounds or even death. The high rate of AIDS among young people is a constant reminder of their mortality. Sexual promiscuity leads to a deluge of sexually transmitted diseases, many incurable. Homicides are the second leading cause of death among fifteen- to twenty-four-year-old males. The Centers for Disease Control reported that youth killings in the United States are ten times higher than in Canada, fifteen times higher than in Australia, and twenty-eight times higher than in Germany or France.[20]

Part of the problem may be that our children are growing up too fast. Psychologist David Elkind argues:

> Society no longer seems to regard children as innocent or to see childhood innocence as a positive characteristic. Children are exposed to every nuance of human vice and

> depravity under the mistaken assumption that this will somehow inure them to evil and prepare them to live successful, if not virtuous and honorable, lives. This assumption rests on the mistaken belief that a bad experience is the best preparation for a bad experience.[21]

Using premarital sex as an example, it seems as though the prevailing attitude of much of our society is that teenagers are going to have sex no matter what we do, so let's not even try to promote abstinence as a solution. The former principal of the high school where my wife works had a saying— "What you permit, you promote." This seems like an invalid commentary to adults with that kind of apathetic attitude regarding many of the problems young people face today.

Boys are also raised with an overabundance of stereotypes they are encouraged to live up to: Men don't cry or express affection. Real men are strong, silent, and able to fix anything. Men don't feel pain. Real men are rich and successful in business. Real men are sexually experienced.

Just look at the myths our male role models perpetuate: James Bond beds every beautiful woman who crosses his path. All of the action movies have larger-than-life heroes who beat up or kill dozens of men at once and never get hurt or die. Our sports, movie, and music stars seemingly get away with any behavior they feel like indulging—drugs, sexual assault, even murder—all without suffering any consequences. What kind of self-image do young boys develop when they feel forced to, or are unable to, live up to these kinds of stereotypes?

Understanding gender differences is crucial in successfully raising boys. At their very core, boys are different than you were as a little girl or are now as a woman. They think, feel, process information, emote, express themselves, and solve problems differently than you do. The following chapters look at these differences, discuss practical skills, and provide encouragement to help solve the problems these differences can create. Mothers who understand these differences have a much better opportunity of reaching their goal of raising boys to become good men.

## Questions for Discussion

1. Make a list of ways your son's behavior differs from yours as a youngster. Which behaviors do you think are a result of his maleness, and which are a result of his environment?
2. What behavioral patterns have you observed that seem consistent with most boys your son's age? Why do you think they act this way?
3. Discuss with another woman or with your group any "anti-boy" atmosphere you've observed in our society.

# 3

# Pitfalls—What to Avoid

My friend swears this is a true story.

Eddie was three years old when his mother taught him to read (her first mistake). One day he was in the bathroom and noticed one of the cabinet doors was ajar. Eddie read the box in the cabinet and asked his mother, "Why are you keeping napkins in the bathroom? Don't they belong in the kitchen?" Not wanting to burden Eddie with unnecessary facts, she told him, "Those napkins are for special occasions."

Fast-forward a few months. It was Thanksgiving Day, and Eddie's folks had left to pick up the pastor and his wife for dinner. Mom had assignments for all of the kids to carry out while they were gone. Eddie's was to set the table.

When they returned, the pastor came in first and immediately burst into laughter. Next came his wife, who gasped and then began giggling. Next came Eddie's father, who roared with laughter. Then came Eddie's mom, who almost died of embarrassment when she saw each place setting on the table with a "special occasion" napkin at each plate, the fork carefully arranged on top. He had even tucked the little "tails" in so they didn't hang off the edge. (This was in the days when sanitary napkins were held in place by clipping the "tails" to a belt.) Eddie's mother asked him why he had used these, and of course, Eddie's response sent the other adults into further fits of laughter. "But, Mom, you *said* they were for special occasions!"

Communication problems aren't the only hurdles mothers face while raising boys. This chapter addresses some of the areas in which mothers raising sons struggle. This is not an exhaustive list but merely some of the pitfalls you should be aware of.

My intent here is not to convict or criticize but rather to point out some areas in which you will want to be sensitive. Hear me clearly: many boys, even those raised by just their mothers, do not have the problems described below. In fact, most boys raised by only their mothers turn out just fine. Simply keep these issues on your radar screen.

## Mothers and Sons and Apron Strings

> Few misfortunes can befall a boy which bring worse consequences than to have a really affectionate mother.
>
> W. Somerset Maugham

Mothers and sons have a special relationship, to be sure. But boys need to break away from their mothers at various stages of life (typically around five years of age and again during adolescence) in order to develop a healthy masculinity. They break away from the tight bond with Mom in various ways. Younger boys will often say insulting things like "You're ugly" or "I hate you" during a tender moment. Comments like these are hurtful to Mom, but they are a boy's way of breaking the tightly wrapped arms of motherhood.[1] Older boys are likely to become disrespectful, sullen, or challenging of your authority (see chapter 6, "Disciplining Boys"). A wise mom, rather than taking these responses personally, understands them to be a stage of normal development and helps guide her son through the process.

Boys growing up in a home where the father is missing or emotionally uninvolved will likely have a harder time becoming independent of their mother. Sometimes a boy's mother stands between him and his being a man. To become a man, a boy must make a clean break from the world of women.

Since the beginning of civilization, tribes around the world have conducted gruesome ceremonies to break boys from the world of women and introduce them into the world of men. Often the boys resist. They'd rather stay in the warm world of women, where they are taken care of and nurtured. But that's not the world of men with its struggles and burdensome responsibilities.[2] After all, our goal is to raise a boy to be a man who is responsible for himself and others around him—a man who nurtures, provides for, protects, and leads his family courageously and accepts responsibility for his own actions. One who, whether married or single, leads nobly in his church, community, and society.

Manhood and fatherhood are learned behaviors. Boys are visual creatures and learn by observing. By watching how men react in certain situations, what they say, and how they solve problems, boys learn to become men. Boys need to be instructed at an early age to take on their manly responsibilities. They need to develop a leadership style that appears both noble to men and endearing to women rather than dominant or abusive. They need to understand a masculine vision of what a real man is. They need a code of conduct teaching them how a real man lives his life. They need a mother *and* a father. If a father is not available, they need a remarkable woman who understands what is necessary to raise a good man.

## But He Might Get Hurt!

> But whether a child is male or female, fathers are needed for their "otherness," to put a healthy wedge between mother and child, to be a haven from real or imagined maternal injustice or excessive hovering.
>
> Victoria Secunda, *Women and Their Fathers*

Chris, a friend of mine, has been dating a single mother with a five-year-old boy. One day I was talking to her about Chris's influence on her son, Tony. She said, "Chris took us to a gravel pit the other day, which was somewhere I would never have thought to take Tony. But he loved it!" She went on, "Chris even let him run to the top of the rock pile. I was sure he would fall and get hurt. I wanted to stop him, but Chris told me no. Chris said that was what made it fun for a boy—the fact that he could get hurt." She pondered for a moment and said, "I never would have thought of that. Tony said it was one of the best days of his life."

John Eldredge, in *Wild at Heart*, says, "The recipe for fun is pretty simple raising boys: Add to any activity an element of danger, stir in a little exploration, add a dash of destruction, and you've got yourself a winner."[3] Sounds reasonable to me.

Mothers, because of their nurturing tendencies, are often overprotective of their children. After all, it's a mother's job to civilize a boy. Without a man's influence in this area, boys can end up failing to learn the valuable link between taking risks and attaining success in life. Getting hurt physically, failing, persevering, and succeeding (despite overwhelming odds) are key factors in a male's growth toward manhood. The boy who's never had a man push him up on the monkey bars and say, "Jump!" suffers, especially if he only has Mom below the monkey bars saying, "Be careful. Take my hand. Don't jump—you might get hurt."[4]

Eldredge says, "I've noticed that so often our word to boys is *don't*. Don't climb on that, don't break anything, don't be so aggressive, don't be so noisy, don't be so messy, don't take such crazy risks. But God's design—which he placed in boys as the picture of himself—is a resounding *yes*. Be fierce, be wild, be passionate."[5]

Even the way a man plays with a young child helps to develop specific portions of the child's brain. By his roughhousing behavior, such as tossing his child in the air, a man signals that it is safe to take risks—provided he catches the child before he hits the ground. Recent studies have shown that men who play with their small children help develop fundamental portions of the children's brains, giving them greater confidence and the ability to take risks throughout life. Louise J. Kaplan says in *Oneness and Separateness: From Infant to Individual,*

> Fathers have a special excitement about them that babies find intriguing. At this time in his life an infant counts on his mother for rootedness and anchoring. He can count on his father to be just different enough from a mother. Fathers embody a delicious mixture of familiarity and novelty. They are novel without being strange or frightening.[6]

The child, especially a boy, learns that risk taking can be fun, rewarding, and sometimes dangerous. Good-natured wrestling on the floor with Dad or other males also promotes physical development, emotional well-being, and self-esteem. Mom, let the boys play, even if someone gets hurt occasionally.

When I was about seven years old, I watched Tarzan on television. Seeing him swing from tree to tree gave me the idea that I could do it too. I climbed up and tied a rope high on a tree branch in our front yard. I grabbed the rope, jumped out, and started to swing. You can guess what happened next. I slid all the way to the ground, the rope burning my hands, shredding all the skin off. Crying, I went running into the house to my mom. Like any good mom in the early 1960s, she spread Vaseline all over my hands, admonished me for doing something so stupid, and sent me out to the front porch to cry myself out. As I sat on the porch sniffling and holding my hands in front of me, the mailman approached.

"What happened to you, son?" he asked.

"I tried to swing on a rope in the tree and hurt my hands," I sobbed, looking for sympathy.

He just looked at me for a moment and shook his head knowingly before whispering, "I'd use gloves next time."

Shazam! What a great idea—gloves! That would keep me from burning my hands and give me a better grip besides.

Notice that he didn't tell me not to do it; he just assumed I would. He knew the rope was something I needed to conquer—to get back up on the horse, so to speak.

Several days later, when my hands were nearly healed, I snuck into the garage and borrowed a pair of my dad's leather work gloves. I climbed the tree, and summoning all my courage, I swung out again. Rapidly I began sliding down the rope. However, on this occasion, I had time to notice that my gloves were burning and my hands were getting hot. I let go. The long fall to the ground, plus landing on my back, knocked the wind out of me. But at least I didn't burn my hands.

You might think by now I'd be getting the picture that this wasn't such a great idea. Sorry, moms; that's not how boys think. This time I didn't tell my mom, as I knew she would ban me from swinging in the tree just when I was about to solve this latest problem. What Mom didn't know wouldn't hurt her.

After recovering, I shook my head and thought about my dilemma. I was stumped. *How in the heck did Tarzan swing on that rope, anyway? He didn't wear gloves.* I decided I had better watch him a little more closely and see if I

**Worst Stunts Pulled by Boys as Reported by Moms**

- Tried to set fire to woodpile located next to garage full of paint cans and gasoline cans.
- Used family home's roof as ramp for skateboard to "see how far we can fly."
- Two-year-old stuck coffee bean up nostril in store, requiring visit to emergency ward to remove.
- Used shopping cart as "rodeo bull" while racing downhill on busy street.
- Tied rope to back of city bus to ski behind on snowy days.
- Ate a sponge, two coins, a worm, cat food, and a rotten potato on a dare.
- Hit little brother on head with hammer while imitating the Three Stooges.
- Tied together multiple fireworks in a can of gasoline to see how big an explosion they could create.
- Painted little brother's face and whole body to look like the Tin Man in *The Wizard of Oz*.
- Two-year-old urinated down heating vent while trying out newly discovered "equipment."

was missing something. During another movie, I suddenly had an epiphany. I noticed that Tarzan wrapped the rope around his foot! Why hadn't I noticed that before? Such a simple thing. Is that what kept him from sliding down the vine?

I ran out to the tree, wrapped my feet in the rope, grabbed on tightly (with gloves), and swung out.

Holy cow! I was swinging free in the wind, just like Tarzan! I bellowed out Tarzan's resounding cry for the whole neighborhood to hear. I imagined myself swinging through the jungle, wrestling lions and rescuing lost maidens.

Of course, eventually it dawned on me that I couldn't get back into the tree and that I was stuck hanging from a rope about twenty feet off the ground. But so what! I could swing on a vine just like Tarzan! Besides, I'd accomplished something that was difficult and had required perseverance, courage, and a good bit of thinking.

That is precisely how boys learn to become men, how they learn to solve life's problems. Don't thwart their efforts by being overly protective. Realize that when boys get hurt, they just consider it plain old bad luck. Mothers who have raised numerous boys often recount tales of their sons jumping off roofs, racing bikes downhill without brakes, making bombs, and generally risking life and limb. It's a wonder sometimes that boys ever live to adulthood.

In fact, be prepared to take your boys to the hospital at least several times while they are growing up. We took my son in for stitches so many times I'm sure the doctors were starting to suspect child abuse. Trying to explain how his dog knocked him down, causing him to hit his head on a rock, or how he picked up a piece of broken glass and cut his thumb throwing it sounded lame even to my ears in the flickering fluorescent lights of the emergency room.

Taking risks is part of growing up to be a man. Your son needs to learn from his failures. A wise mother lets her son be a boy. She'll be blessed throughout her life because of it.

## Smothering with Love

Breaking free from the delicious security of mother love can be a painful rupture for either mother or son. Some

> boys can't do it. Some mothers can't let it happen because they know the boy is not ready to leave her; others are simply not ready to give up their sons.
>
> Frank Pittman, *Man Enough*

Some mothers, in an effort to fill the void created by the lack of male leadership in the home, either become domineering or smother boys with mother love. Adolescent-aged and older males caught in these situations can, and often do, rebel in one of two ways. They either become angry and seek to dominate women or they become feminized.

If a mother hopes to promote her son's healthy growth, she must learn to respect his maleness. Don't let your relationship with your son get swallowed up by bitterness, no matter how genuine your grievance against the male gender. Again, not all boys raised by their mothers react in these rebellious ways. However, enough young men are reacting in these ways that it bears a closer look.

Robert Lewis in his excellent tape series, *A Journey into Authentic Manhood,* talks about what happens when boys are raised in an all-female world. I recommend that these tapes be required listening for all young men. Several of the sessions discuss what Lewis calls the "overly bonded with Mother wound." He describes this as "an unhealthy emotional bond between a mother and son, not purposefully inflicted, that stunts or inhibits a healthy masculinity." This happens when a well-intentioned mom, seeing the vacuum left in her son's life by a physically or emotionally absent father, rushes in to save the day. In her desire to rescue her son, Mom goes too far. In these instances, she

**Boy-Friendly Things to Say in Public**

| Instead of Saying: | Consider Saying: |
|---|---|
| "I love you." | "Great catch last night!" |
| "Be careful—don't hurt yourself." | "Try not to end up in the hospital again." |
| "Does that hurt?" | "You must be tough as nails!" |
| "How do you feel about that?" | "I remember once when I . . ." |
| "Why are you feeling bad?" | "Can you help me fix this?" |

bonds too deeply, becoming emotionally overinvolved, treating her son as a surrogate husband, and inadvertently recasts her son's sexual identity. While Lewis describes the "fatherless wound" as a jagged, gaping wound, he describes the "mother wound" as a subtle, fine razor cut. The reason? It's disguised as love, not abuse. Who doesn't want love? What boy, especially one who has been abandoned by his father, wouldn't want excessive love and care showered upon him?[7]

In the movie *About a Boy*, Hugh Grant plays an aging bachelor who decides to target single "mums" for his sexual peccadilloes. But the movie is really about a young boy's desire and need for older male companionship. Marcus, the twelve-year-old son of a depressed single mother, desperately needs the assurance and guidance of a man in his life, and seems to know it intuitively. Marcus wears feminine clothing, has a more feminized haircut, and is passive in school. In one of the movie's key scenes, his mother walks him to school and spontaneously shouts across the playground, "Marcus, I love you!" This, of course, elicits a chorus of teasing and insults from the other children. His mother, who obviously loves her son very much, is oblivious to the fragile needs of his budding manliness. Other scenes in the movie touch on a man's instinctive understanding of a boy's struggles and needs, as well as the reassurance a boy gets from an older male.

Remember, though, that a mother is perhaps the most influential person in a boy's life. Boys learn early in life not to disrespect another male's mother at risk of physical harm. Your tough little boy still needs his mother's love and affection, just not so much in public.

Boys raised mainly under the supervision of women—Mom, female teachers, female Sunday school teachers, female Cub Scout leaders—often experience insecurity over their identity as men. The problem continues when young men leave home. Universities now require women's studies, which typically demonize masculine behavior.[8] How are boys raised in close proximity to only women supposed to learn anything other than female responses to life situations? Carl Jung said that when a son is introduced to feelings primarily by the mother, he will learn the female attitude toward masculinity and take a female view of his own father and of his own masculinity.

A novel of psychological suspense by Andrew Klavan called *Man and Wife* addresses the confusion experienced by a young man who has never had a positive male role model. Peter, a troubled nineteen-year-old young man, is talking to his psychiatrist about his struggles understanding what being a man is all about:

> "To be a man is a surprisingly complicated thing it turns out," he went on softly. "You would think you could just do it but . . . I don't know. I think about it a lot. I guess I don't feel very—*manly*. I never really have. And I've always

> felt—bad about that. *Really* bad. I still feel bad about it. But then, you know, when I think about it? I'm not even sure what it is. To be a man. I mean, what is it? Everyone tells you what it's not—that it's not swaggering around or punching people—that's what they say anyway—but . . . I think maybe if my father had stayed—maybe I could just look at him and say, 'That's what it's like. That's what it means. That's what a man is.' But without that . . . it's just such an abstraction to me. It's like I wrack my brains—what is it, what is it? And then other guys, they just seem to know. Without even thinking. Sometimes I look at some guy—even if he's some kind of absolute [jerk], you know—I look at him and I envy him. I sit there and envy him because he just seems to know how to be a man. . . ."
>
> Peter went on, "The trouble is, the only people who ever talk about manhood are people who don't know. Because part of being a man is not having to talk about it. Women—I mean, you can't trust women on this at all. They lie, for one thing. They'll tell you they think a man should be gentle or considerate or some stuff. But all they really want is a man who's a real man. They'd rather have him manly and kind if they can get it—at least, I guess they would—but they'll take him manly and cruel if they have to. Or they'll take him kind and wish he were manly and spend their lives dreaming about that. But if you ask them what that is—to be manly, to be a man, they start babbling and lying about it—because they don't really know! Because it's an abstraction that some men understand in their hearts but women don't because they're women."[9]

Peter, like many young men today who are raised only by women, is struggling with his masculine identity. Boys raised under these circumstances often react in one of two ways.

The first reaction is to overidentify with women and become feminized. Not effeminate, but feminized. The feminized man can be a football star or race car driver—on the outside he's a real man's man, but inside he has developed traits more typically associated with the female gender, such as passivity and indecisiveness. He tends to identify with the overabundant female mentors who are authorities in his life. He tends to be passive in social relationships. Have you ever noticed that many men today want women to call them, instead of vice versa? They don't take risks or initiate anything. They're happy to sit back and let women come to them, to serve them. They also can't or won't make a decision about a permanent relationship. They lack decisiveness—they can't even decide which restaurant or movie to attend.[10]

Here's a common scenario around our house that illustrates female passivity and indecisiveness. My wife and I are planning to go out to dinner.

I say, "Where do you want to go eat?"

Suzanne says, "I don't care. You decide."

"How about Tony Roma's?"

"No, ribs are too messy."

"Okay, how about The Olive Garden?"

"No, we just ate there."

"Well, how about Chinese, then?"

"No, I don't feel like Chinese."

Slightly exasperated, I say, "Well, where *do* you want to eat?"

To which my wife replies, "I don't care. You choose."

Men who have become feminized often have the same difficulty making decisions.

Feminized men, whom Robert Bly calls "soft males," place a greater emphasis on feelings than on convictions. They resist when they don't *feel* like doing something.[11]

Part of boys growing up and becoming men is learning to do things they don't want to when they don't want to. Feminized men need group approval before committing. These men are afraid of making decisions and shun risks. They become dependent on women to take care of them, to make all the decisions for them. That's how they've been raised.

One of the unfortunate traits of a feminized man is that when he looks for a mate, he marries someone like Mom—usually a strong woman who will make decisions and take care of him. Of course, his wife thinks this is great—at first. She's marrying a sensitive man with feelings, after all. But she soon becomes frustrated with having to make all the decisions. The more she pushes him, the more passive he becomes. The more passive and indecisive he becomes, the more frustrated she gets, eventually losing all respect for him.

The second reaction of boys who are raised only by women is to become macho and aggressive toward women, to rebel against female leadership. The rebel will be overly assertive, especially about his sexual prowess. He doesn't want women controlling him—he's in control! He's dominant in his authority. He tends to have children with multiple partners, usually abandoning them all. He can be physically and emotionally abusive as well.[12]

In her book *Between Mothers and Sons: The Making of Vital and Loving Men*, Evelyn Bassoff, Ph.D., writes, "In fatherless homes and communities, young boys are not helped by men to separate from their mothers. An unbroken dependence on and closeness with mother can lead to rage against her and all women . . . or create a hyper masculinity characterized by excessive aggressiveness."[13]

Look at some of the young men around you, even at some of the men with whom you've been involved. Do any of the characteristics of either of these two types of men seem familiar? These shadow men are becoming more and more pervasive in our fatherless culture.

## No Quitting!

> Never, never, never, never give up!
>
> Winston Churchill

When my son, Frank, was in sixth grade, he decided he wanted to go out for the middle school wrestling team. I had wrestled all through high school, so I knew what he would be getting himself into. Now, don't get me wrong. My son is a great kid, but he doesn't have a mean bone in his body.

After we discussed some of the harder aspects of wrestling, such as exercising vigorously, practicing constantly, watching your weight, and getting slammed to the floor repeatedly, he decided he still wanted to try out. I have a firm rule with my kids: I don't care what they attempt, but they must stick with it for a reasonable amount of time—usually a season. So Frank headed off to the wrestling team.

Frank was heavy for his age, and since wrestlers are divided by weight classes, he naturally ended up wrestling eighth graders most of the time in practice. There can be a huge difference in muscle mass between sixth-grade and eighth-grade boys. Many eighth graders have been through puberty and have developed manlike muscles. Two weeks into the season, Frank wanted to quit the team. He was getting hurt by the older boys in practice. It got to the point where he was coming home bruised and battered, crying and saying, "They're hurting me. I just don't want to be hurt anymore!" It broke my heart to look into Frank's teary eyes and tell him he couldn't quit. He was going to have to suck it up and be a man, to finish what he started. I prayed to God many times to confirm that I was doing the right thing. To make matters worse, my wife was giving me "the look." You know that look. The one that says, "You had better know what you're doing, buddy. That's my child you're messing with. You're going to be in big trouble if this goes badly."

To make a long story short, I made Frank stay on the team. In his first wrestling contest, he was matched against a young fellow bigger than he was but about his own age and maturity level. During the first two rounds and most of the third, Frank was tossed around the mat like a chew toy in the jaws of a puppy. His main strategy was to adopt a turtlelike posture on his belly—probably a learned defense mechanism from wrestling older, bigger boys in practice. Survival was his only goal. However, at the very end of the match, his opponent, exhausted from pushing Frank's weight around the mat, inexplicably dropped and rolled over onto his back. Frank looked up in surprise, fell on top of him, and pinned him! Suddenly Frank's whole countenance changed. He jumped up and danced around the ring on his toes with his arms in the air.

As he looked at me across the gym, he knew that the hours of hard work and pain had paid off. The reward was his because he had not quit when the going was tough. And the reward was that much sweeter—like cool, clear water, refreshing his soul—because of the agonies he'd endured.

We soon discovered, however, that we had created a monster. Frank went on to pin his next seven opponents before finally coming back down to earth. He never wrestled again after that season, but it provided him with several valuable lessons he'll remember his whole life—hard work is its own reward, persistence and perseverance are rewarded, and finish what you start.

A man's role in life often requires him to persist in the face of adversity. This valuable skill is lost when boys are allowed to quit. Mothers need to understand that a boy who learns to quit during hard times will be more likely to give up on his own wife and children when the going gets tough. Eldredge says, "Life needs a man to be fierce—and fiercely devoted. The wounds he will take throughout his life will cause him to lose heart if all he has been trained to be is soft. This is especially true in the murky waters of relationships, where a man feels least prepared to advance."[14]

Don't misunderstand me. I'm not saying there are never appropriate times to allow boys to quit an activity. But quitting can easily become a lifelong habit if allowed to happen too often. I see too many boys and young men today who have acquired the habit of quitting. Perseverance is one of the qualities a stint in the military instills in young men.

It's pretty hard to quit—and the going gets plenty tough during boot camp and throughout a tour of duty.

Nothing great was ever accomplished by quitting. Push boys to strive to do great things. Give them a dream to look toward. Boys need dreams. Dreams also give them hope—hope that they too can one day stand in the footsteps of men who have achieved greatness.

## Questions for Discussion

1. In what ways have you been overprotective of your son? Talk to a man you trust (your husband, father, grandfather, uncle, pastor, or your son's father) to see what he thinks.
2. In what areas in your relationship with your son do you feel you might be overinvolved?
3. Have you ever allowed your son to quit something he started? Have you regretted that decision? Why or why not?

# 4

# Boys and Sex

> We use a most unfortunate idiom when we say, of a lustful man prowling the streets, that he "wants a woman." Strictly speaking, a woman is just what he does not want. He wants a pleasure for which a woman happens to be the necessary piece of apparatus. How much he cares about the woman as such may be gauged by his attitude to her five minutes after fruition (one does not keep the carton after one has smoked the cigarettes).
>
> *C. S. Lewis,* The Four Loves

## How Males Think about Sex

As with most things in life, men and women tend to view sex from differing perspectives. God created both men and women as sexual beings—yet differently. If you remember our discussion earlier about the hormone testosterone and its effects on the male body and psyche, you can begin to understand why and how some of these differences manifest themselves. While at first glance some of the things I'm about to say may seem shocking or even somewhat repulsive, please remember that males have been purposefully wired the way they are by our heavenly Father. Thus, the daily struggles boys and men encounter with lust should be viewed with compassion, grace, and understanding, particularly toward those males who choose to keep sexuality and sexual impulses within God-given boundaries.

At the risk of perpetuating a stereotype about men, there's a distinct possibility that if women knew how and what men really think about, they would refuse to be in the same room with them (I use the term *men*, but it's interchangeable with *boys* from early adolescence on). They'd think them perverted. Guys think about sex all the time. Men even think about sex in the most inappropriate places, such as in church or at funerals. The slightest and most innocent thing—a woman's laugh, the curve of a shapely leg, certain shoes, perfume, and thousands of other scents, sights, and sounds—can set men off. During adolescence, when hormones are raging, these stimulations are intensified.

Males can also be stimulated by nothing—for no reason at all. They can become aroused purely as a physical function of their sex. Stephen Arterburn and Fred Stoeker, in *Every Man's Battle*, make the following insightful (or exasperating, depending on your point of view) statement: "The human male, because of sperm production and other factors, naturally desires sexual release about every forty-eight to seventy-two hours."[1] That's every two to three days. (I'm trying to convince my wife of the validity of this statistic, but she suspects I've made it up.)

Dr. Kevin Leman, author of *Making Sense of the Men in Your Life*, says this about men:

> Another thing women just don't understand is what it means when I say men are physical beings. We are *attracted* to the physical. . . . I'm not trying to shock you here, but I want to open up your eyes to a truth that often gets glossed over. I want you to think of a man you most admire and trust, and he must be a nonrelative. . . . You got this guy in your mind? Good. Now put yourself in a position where you're meeting this man in a social situation. In less than one-fifth of a second, this man has checked you out from your toes to your head and *all* the major spots in between.[2]

And that myth I hear from women all the time that a man is "just a friend," that "he's not physically attracted to me"? Sorry, that's just not true. Sexuality permeates all of a man's relationships to one degree or another. A man may say he's not sexually interested in a woman, that he's just friends with her, but he knows in his heart he's lying. And every other man, if honest, knows he's lying as well. A good man will control his feelings and impulses toward a woman to whom he's not married, but that doesn't mean that those feelings and impulses are not still there. A man who hangs around helping out whenever he can for no other reason than that he is your "friend" is sexually attracted to you no matter what he says to the contrary. Men don't tend to do many things that aren't in their own self-interest.

That males think about sex a lot may not be press-stopping news to some of you, but the depth of how it impacts their everyday lives might come as a surprise. Even young boys become preoccupied with sex. I remember at age eight playing "doctor" under the porch with neighbor girls at every opportunity. Men reportedly think about sex an average of thirty-three times per day, or twice an hour. Some people say women think about sex only once a day—when men ask for it.[3] You can imagine how distracting sex can be for males when they spend so much time and energy thinking about it.

If sex is not the first thing on a man's mind, it is certainly always lurking around in the background waiting to spring forward and pounce. Lust is a constant struggle, and those males who choose to live a life of sexual purity face a mighty battle. I am convinced that most women do not understand the intensity of that battle, primarily because women are not as visually stimulated as men. Women are more aroused by physical touch and relationships. A man is instantly aroused merely by the glimpse of a female body or parts thereof. That's why it is important for girls and women to understand the importance of how they dress. When women really understand the degree of struggle lust represents in a male's life, they are generally more compassionate than disgusted with the male preoccupation with sex.

A woman is fertile approximately three hundred times during her lifetime. During times of ovulation, her sex hormones increase as a biological response to make her seek a mate. Many women notice an increased interest in sex during this time. Just imagine the adolescent male receiving seven to ten shots of these increases per *day*. That will give you some idea of the struggle he faces with sexual impulses.[4]

Now that you have an inkling of some of the challenges your growing son faces, how can you help him to not only be aware of but actually deal with the coming battle in a productive manner? Let's start by examining some of the minefields in the journey from boyhood to manhood.

## Sex Education

Many parents leave the sexual education of their kids to the schools. I suspect that's because it's an uncomfortable topic for discussion. It wouldn't surprise me if most moms are somewhat intimidated by discussing sex with their sons. But if you start early and can become comfortable discussing sexual issues before puberty sets in, you might just be the best person to introduce him to his sexuality. In his book *What a Difference a Daddy Makes,* Dr. Kevin Leman suggests that fathers should be the primary sex educators for their daughters, and mothers for their sons. As he says:

> Who better knows what a man needs than another man? In the same way, who better can explain a woman's perspective on sexuality than a boy's mom? Look, little Joey already understands what it feels like to have a penis! What he doesn't know, but really wants to know, is how it feels to have two breasts, how girls react to boys, and

> how he can relate to the opposite sex without making a total fool of himself.[5]

Certainly, there are areas of a boy's sexuality that are more appropriate for him to discuss with a man. But a mom can play a hugely important role in developing her son's healthy sexuality and, especially as he gets older, teaching him how to relate to a young lady's needs. Girls really are mysterious to boys. The more information a boy has on how females think, feel, and act, the more comfortable and confident he will be in his relationships.

Some of the simplest truths that you take for granted may not be evident to your son. For instance, boys might not understand without being told that it hurts for a girl to have her breast grabbed and that girls really don't think very highly of that particular act. Also, if boys understood the sensitive nature of girls at specific ages, they might be less likely to say things that deeply wound a young girl.

Don't be afraid to relate some of your experiences as a young woman. Tell your son how you felt during various situations and what you wished you had done differently. If you really want to make a difference in your son's life, you must spend time talking with him about these subjects. Leman says, "If you want your son to pick up how to relate to women from you rather than sixteen-year-old Sally down the street, you have to ask yourself: *Am I willing to spend as much time with him as Sally is?*"[6]

Give your son practical advice. Boys have no clue how to properly ask a girl out or how to act on a date. Teach your

**Discussing Sex Education with Your Children**

Start discussing sex with your children early. Treat the topic matter-of-factly. Don't wait until your children ask about sex. Answer their questions directly and honestly. Use proper names such as *penis* or *vagina* instead of cute slang terms. Use age-appropriate books, movies, and television shows to facilitate discussions. Respect your children's privacy and teach them to respect others' privacy. Don't brush off or ignore your children's questions about sex. Repeat explanations.

| Age: | Topics: |
|---|---|
| Preschool | Don't punish children for touching their own genitalia.<br>Explain what private parts are and what privacy means.<br>Explain sex differences. |
| Grade School | Discuss issues of procreation in age-appropriate, general terms.<br>Discuss menstruation with girls before they enter adolescence.<br>Discuss masturbation in general terms with boys at a relatively early age. |
| Adolescent | Teach responsibility and self-control.<br>Teach that sex is not just intercourse.<br>Teach that sexual intimacy has profound consequences.<br>Teach that it's okay to say no to sex until they're married.<br>Teach that sex is not the most important part of a loving relationship.[7] |

son table manners. Talk to him about some of the character qualities young women admire in young men. Lastly, even if it is uncomfortable, be sure to keep the lines of communication open with your son in the area of sex.

## Pornography

I tell mothers all the time not to be overprotective of their sons. Pornography, however, is an area in which I urge overprotectiveness. Pornography is the most destructive force men and boys face today. It is irresistible primarily due to males' visual nature. Studies have shown that pornography works in the same stimulation centers of the brain in men that cocaine does and has the same addictive capabilities. Pornography triggers the release of a hormone that etches erotic images in a man's mind like the developing process etches a photograph on Kodak paper. This hormone creates a high and causes the user to want more.

These images stay with a man for the rest of his life, desensitizing him toward women and causing him to make unfair and unrealistic comparisons. No real female can compete with the airbrushed images of women who've had professionally done makeup and hairstyling and the aid of photographers.

When I was growing up, about the only venue for pornography was stealing *Playboy* magazine from one of my friends' dads. By today's standards, *Playboy* is tame. Much of the programming currently on network television is more graphic in nature than anything that appeared in *Playboy* in the mid-1960s. Today boys and men are bombarded with a constant barrage of sexually graphic images. Everywhere males turn, sex is being shoved in their faces. Everything from Victoria's Secret advertisements to unsolicited pornographic website spam is in your son's face from the time he wakes up until he sleeps at night. Even the department store advertisements in the newspaper and on billboards are quite titillating. Sex sells, and Madison Avenue is quick to push the boundaries at every opportunity in order to get our money. If that requires addicting boys to pornography at a young age, so be it.

The reality is that pornography degrades women. Pornography makes victims of both the viewer and the viewee. The only ones who profit are those who sell it. It turns women into objects to be played with, property to be bought and sold. It makes the user think women like rape, torture, and humiliation.

Porn also diminishes sexual fulfillment in men. It breeds discontent in their lives on many levels. Porn users need bigger prizes—more degrading, more graphic, more explicit images.

The many times I've cautioned my son and other boys about the dangers of pornography, I've tried to put it in its proper perspective. The women involved in those pictures and videos are someone's daughters and sisters. Someday they might be some child's mommy. Would he like men lusting and fantasizing about his sister or mother like he fantasizes about the women in the porn? Also, by viewing this material, a male is not exercising self-restraint or control. If he can't use self-control in one area of his life, he'll lack it in other areas as well. Boys who learn to govern their sexual urges grow up to be men who are able to engage in healthy sexual relations and are able to control other areas of their lives.

Lastly, pornography disenfranchises a man's wedding vows, causing him to live in continual adultery. This applies even if he's not married. Jesus says in Matthew 5:28,

"Whoever looks at a woman to lust for her has already committed adultery with her in his heart." Pornography is sin. It destroys our relationship with God. The good news is that a man can find cleansing and forgiveness through God's grace.

Your son can access free pornography any time he wants, day or night—lewd images you probably can't even imagine. Jealously guard your computers and the television. Use Internet protection software on your computer, and program the cable parental controls on your television to block channels boys shouldn't be watching. Don't think, *My son would never look at that filth.* Sorry, Mom, but yes, he would, even at a young age. He won't be able to help himself.

Help protect your son from this scourge of manhood; err on the side of caution in this area.

### Masturbation

Masturbation is one of the more uncomfortable topics for me to talk about in front of a group of women. Quite frankly, it's not even very comfortable to write about. However, I believe it is such an important subject that it needs to be discussed. So despite my embarrassment, I forge ahead during my seminars and talk about masturbation. Surprisingly, the majority of the women in attendance are very curious and open to learning more about a male's perspective on this somewhat taboo subject.

Understandably, many moms are uncomfortable dealing with their son's sexuality. And many, if not most, women I've known seem to have a strong reaction toward the subject of masturbation. Moms have been known to freak out when confronted with this act. Anyone over the age of forty remembers being raised with the admonition that you would go blind or grow hair on your palms if you indulged in this act. That puritanical attitude still lingers in the back of many people's subconscious.

Frequent masturbation by boys is normal during adolescence. There's an old joke that says studies have shown that 98 percent of boys masturbate—and the other 2 percent lie about it. It might be an old joke, but it's one that is true. In fact, it is normal for even very young males to like to rub or touch themselves. A boy's penis is a big part of his life. It can provide exquisite pleasure or, if hit, great pain. He handles it every time he goes to the bathroom or bathes. As Dr. Leman says, "It's always there, a little companion that every boy meets, stares at—and usually plays with—several times a day."[8]

I would even go so far as to say that it is virtually impossible that an adolescent male will not engage in masturbation at least periodically, despite his moral upbringing or the most stringent efforts at willpower. Likely, the more pressure that's put on a young man not to indulge in this act, the more he's apt to. The reason? He thinks about it all the more often.

While masturbation is certainly a private activity, excessive disapproval of this natural inclination produces an unhealthy guilt, which can affect a man's sexual attitude for a lifetime. Teaching boys the value of self-control in this area without making them feel guilty is imperative.

Masturbation in young males absolutely should not be ridiculed or even made an issue. A friend of mine still feels humiliation twenty years later as he recalls his mother joking to a mixed-gender crowd of his friends that she was glad he had finally moved out of the house—she wouldn't have to contend with the stains on his sheets anymore. That mother left an unhealthy sexual legacy for her son that affects him to this day.

Another sometimes unsettling occurrence in the sexual development of adolescent boys takes place in the form of nocturnal emissions. This is where a young man has a sexually graphic dream that causes him to ejaculate in his sleep. These emissions are normal and are not something he can control. These dreams act as a pressure relief valve for the sexual psyche. Your son will likely be embarrassed, if not horrified, when something like this happens for the first time. In addition, the first emission or two may contain blood, which is very frightening if a boy is not prepared beforehand.

Wise mothers understand and learn about the sexual development stages boys go through and take these episodes in stride when they happen, explaining that they are a normal part of growing up.

### The Dating Game

At what age should boys begin dating? Certainly, many books have been written by people much wiser than myself on this subject. However, I believe the age of dating is a subjective, family-specific decision based on the teen's maturity and the level of responsibility he has shown. My son, Frank, and several of his teenage friends, both male and female, have read Joshua Harris's excellent book *I Kissed Dating Goodbye*. That book caused each of them to make the decision to hold off on dating until at least after high school, perhaps longer. My daughter, Kelsey, upon hearing this, instantly refused to read the book out of fear that she too would be "brainwashed."

The summer before she entered high school, Kelsey and I went on a weeklong road trip by ourselves. The trip was ostensibly to talk about high school, but I used it to talk about all the things she didn't want to know—things like what teenage boys really want and how they think. She didn't want to hear those things, but being trapped in a car together, crossing remote areas of eastern Washington, allowed me to ramble on at will. The trip also allowed us to agree on some ground rules for the coming school year.

One of the things we settled on was that Kelsey would not date during her freshman year. Coming from a small private Christian school, this would allow her to get her feet on the ground and settle into public high school life. Kelsey honored our agreement this past year with remarkably little resistance or complaining. I think she found it useful to be able to use Dad as an excuse to turn down the myriad of boys who descended upon her. It also allowed her to observe how boys react and how they think without the pressure of a relationship.

This year she will be able to slowly begin dating, starting out with group dates and then double-dating. This again allows her to gain experience without finding herself in an awkward position in which she must make a tough decision without the benefit of having been there before.

We also agreed that Kelsey will not call boys on the telephone but may receive calls from them. Boys need to learn to take the initiative in relationships and not be passive. Also, she cannot date seniors until she is at least a junior. It is my opinion that boys at that age level are much too sophisticated in their manipulative abilities for young, inexperienced girls to deal with. Older girls at school warned her at the beginning of the year that senior boys often target freshman girls for sexual exploitation because of their naïveté.

Frank and his friends have decided to break into the dating scene rather cautiously. A large group of boys and girls from his youth group at church attend different events together, allowing relationships to grow slowly while learning about the differences between the genders—again without the pressures of dating.

There's some pretty clear evidence from a variety of studies that show that the longer a teenager (boy or girl) holds off before beginning dating, the greater the chance he or she will remain sexually pure until marriage. We've learned from teenage pregnancies that children cannot mother and father their own children. As each of us knows, it's a natural human response to want to achieve a greater level of satisfaction every time we do something. This is especially true during physical experiences, such as with drugs or sex. If we kiss a girl on one date, we want to go a little farther each and every time. Also, as each barrier breaks down, it becomes morally easier to go beyond the next time. I see moms who think it's cute that their twelve-year-old daughters are starting to date. But if young people are dating and kissing at age twelve, what will they be doing by the time they're fourteen, fifteen, or sixteen years old?

Discuss with your son the need to make decisions about his personal behavioral boundaries before he's faced with a tough choice. If he knows his boundaries ahead of time, it is easier than trying to make decisions in the "heat of battle." The backseat of a car in the throes of passion is not a good place to decide whether or not he is going to remain sexually pure. Additionally, if he has made life choice decisions beforehand, he's not as likely to find himself in a position that requires him to make difficult choices.

Dr. James Dobson, in his fantastic book for adolescents titled *Preparing for Adolescence*, talks about the importance of making those kinds of decisions beforehand and then cementing them by creating pacts with a group of friends—sort of an accountability staff. For instance, if your son decides to remain sexually pure until marriage, he needs to express that to a group of like-minded friends who all make a pact together. This creates a supportive peer group and a form of accountability. If a friend sees another friend in a situation or relationship that will potentially compromise his pact, he can call him to account.[9]

Many of my friends who have teenage daughters make it a practice to interview the young men they date before entrusting their daughters to their care. Dennis Rainey describes one such experience:

> When our oldest daughter, Ashley, was 16 she was allowed to date. But I made it clear I wanted to interview any boys who asked her out.
>
> I still remember that first interview. Kevin showed up at my office riding his motorcycle (?!). I bought him a soft drink to keep things as informal as possible, and then, after several minutes of small talk, I looked him in the eye.

"You know, Kevin, I was a teenage boy once," I said. "And I want you to know that I remember what the sex drive is like for an 18-year-old young man." His eyes were getting bigger—he was really listening.

"I expect you to treat my daughter just like God would have you treat His finest creation—with all respect and dignity. Whether you go out with her one time or 100 times, I want to be able to look you in the eyes and ask you if you are treating my daughter with respect and dignity—especially in the physical area. God may want her to be another man's wife, so you better be very careful to keep this relationship pure."

On my way home I wondered if I was being too intrusive. Then over dinner my doubts evaporated when I shared what had happened.

It wasn't just Ashley's response of appreciation. It was Benjamin, who was 14 at the time, who put it all in context. He said, "You know, Dad, I hope that the father of a girl I ask out wants to meet with me. I'll know I'm at the right house if that happens!"

The reason I met with Kevin is that I believe Barbara and I, as parents, have been entrusted by God to protect our children's innocence. I'm convinced that parents need to possess a godly jealousy that ruthlessly protects our children from evil.[10]

Boys and girls mature at remarkably different rates. Several years ago I was a consultant with Junior Achievement, where I taught one hour a week in an eighth-grade class for the entire year. I observed that many of the girls' physical development was that of a typical twenty-year-old, while most of the boys were only chest high to the girls and looked about eight years old. When did girls start developing so early? I looked back at my old high school yearbook at the girls I remember as being "built." I was shocked to see that by today's standards they looked like scrawny little grade-schoolers.

I also observed these very mature girls figuratively leading these immature little boys around by the nose, playing flirting games the boys didn't understand in the slightest. In the halls of the high school where my wife works, girls may be observed kissing their much smaller counterparts in the halls. They look like women with their pets. Many of the boys wear a panicked look, realizing they are in over their heads. Unfortunately, due to peer pressure and natural male ego, they cannot refuse the girls' advances.

While I've joked with my teenage daughter that boys are like dogs—they run around in packs marking their territory and sniffing after females—I think younger teenage boys are much more reluctant to engage in physical relationships than girls are. Boys are unsure of how to act in a relationship, and girls scare them. Unfortunately, television and the movies seem to equate maturity in boys with sexual experience.

Obviously, as boys mature (usually later in high school), they catch up with the girls and become the aggressors. It's their nature. Many young men, without proper guidance, will do or say anything to get into a young lady's pants. Boys need to understand that they have a responsibility in physical relationships—it's not just the girl's job to say no.

Talk to your son about his impending sexuality. Begin at an early age and keep the door open as he gets older. Often, the best way to get boys to talk is not to lecture them but to use your life experiences as examples. Also, look for opportunities to facilitate healthy discussions. I had been struggling with trying to talk with my then ten-year-old son about sex in general and masturbation in particular. As my son and I were returning from his first Boy Scout camping trip, the perfect opportunity presented itself. My son was required to read the first few pages of the Scout's handbook with his parent. These pages discussed protecting yourself from sexual molestation and abuse. As my son read these pages aloud, it gave rise to questions he had and opened the door to discussions that made the job of introducing him to his impending sexuality all that much easier.

## Questions for Discussion

1. Have you thought of how you want to protect your children in the sexual area when they become teenagers? What guidelines will you set?
2. Talk to your son about sex, particularly about how females view sex and relationships. Even if it's uncomfortable, talk about the changes his body will undergo as he goes through adolescence, as well as the changes girls experience.
3. Discuss with another woman how pornography has affected her life and what measures she currently takes to keep it from impacting her household.

# 5

# Communicating with Boys

"Bobby, turn down the television.
"Bobby, did you hear me?
"Bobby, I'm not going to tell you again. Turn down the television.
"Bobby! If you don't turn that TV down, you're gonna get it.
"BOBBY! TURN DOWN THE TV! NOW!"
"Huh? Oh, sorry, Mom. I didn't hear you."

Does that sound familiar? Why can boys hear the ice cream truck from a mile away but can't hear you tell them from across the room not to slam the screen door?

Boys only have about a thirty-second attention span. They literally cannot hear things that don't interest them. Frankly, they don't bother listening most of the time anyway. Some of this short attention span is due to the fact that they focus intently on things that interest them. Part of the problem may be that their minds are somewhere else, and part of it could be that they know Mom will tell them again anyway.

To communicate with your son, it's important to understand how the male mind works. For thousands of years, a man's main role in life was to hunt to provide food for his family. Besides strong problem-solving skills, what are two of the main requirements to be a successful hunter? The ability to be silent and the ability to focus intently on one thing. These two traits have been bred into men for ages. Unfortunately, those traits don't always correlate with clear communication between males and females.[1] Our culture makes so many demands on our attention. The sheer noisiness of our society makes it hard for men to concentrate on more than one task at a time.

Males value power, competency, efficiency, and achievement.[2] They are more interested in objects and things than in people and feelings. Achieving goals helps a male feel competent and good about himself. And men like attaining their goals on their own. Autonomy is a symbol of efficiency, power, and competency. However, when teaching your son things like communication skills, resist the urge to do too much for him.

Solving all of your son's dilemmas for him does not enable him to develop a key ingredient of the male psyche—the ability to solve problems. John Gray, in *Men Are from Mars, Women Are from Venus,* states, "To offer a man unsolicited advice is to presume that he doesn't know what to do or that he can't do it on his own. Men are very touchy about this, because the issue of competence is so very important to them. . . . Asking for help when you can do it yourself is perceived as a sign of weakness."[3] Understanding this male characteristic makes it easier to comprehend why your son shows frustration when you offer him advice or continually tell him what to do and how to do things.

So how are you supposed to communicate with your boy, especially in light of the fact that most males view talking as a burden, not a cure? Here are a number of key factors that may make it easier for you to understand the way your son thinks and to communicate with him on a level he can understand.

## Males Can't Read Minds

This parable arrived in my email one day:

> A man asked his wife what she'd like for her 40th birthday.
>
> "I'd love to be six again," she replied.
>
> On the morning of her birthday, he got her up bright and early and off they went to a local theme park. What a day! He put her on every ride in the park: the Death Slide, the Screaming Loop, the Wall of Fear, everything there was! Wow!
>
> Five hours later she staggered out of the theme park, her head reeling and her stomach upside down. Right to a McDonald's they went, where her husband ordered her a Happy Meal along with extra fries and a refreshing chocolate shake. Then, it was off to a movie—the latest Disney and what a fabulous adventure!
>
> Finally, she wobbled home with her husband and collapsed into bed. He leaned over and lovingly asked, "Well, dear, what was it like being six again?"
>
> One eye opened. "You idiot, I meant SIZE 6!!"

The moral of this story: when a woman speaks and a man is actually listening, he will still get it wrong.

I once spoke to a man from a tiny village in Nigeria. He said the first advice his grandfather taught him when he got married was to just say, "Yes, dear." All over the world, men struggle to understand and communicate with women.

Yes, I know. If we men really loved you women, we'd be perceptive to your wants and anticipate your needs. Every male in the world has heard that proclamation. Unfortunately, that's not how males think. We process information with one side of the brain at a time.

Males likely won't understand what you want if you don't tell them directly. Boys need you to speak in their language, with a certain frankness and toughness. Have you ever seen a dog cock his head and whine in confusion when you talk to him? He's trying to understand what you're saying, but he just can't quite grasp the meaning. That's how we feel. We want to make you happy; we just don't understand.

From a male's perspective, women seem to talk in riddles. They hear women "talk around" a subject without seeming to get to the point. That confuses males. We need to know what's expected of us, and how long it will take, in order to feel comfortable and more easily process what's been said. Getting my wife to let us know when she is changing topics has been a big help for me and my son in being able to follow along better when she is talking to us.

Here's an example of female riddle-speak. My wife and I are driving down the highway. Things are going along just fine until she says, "That's an interesting-looking antique shop we just passed."

I say, "Yup."

Silence permeates the interior of the car, and we continue down the road.

Twenty miles later, my senses start tingling and I detect something is wrong. All of a sudden, out of nowhere, I'm trying to figure out why my wife's mad at me.

"It's because you didn't stop at the antique store like I asked you to," she snarls.

Now, in my steel-trap mind, I'm doing several things. First, I'm trying to figure out *what* antique store she's talking about. And second, I'm trying to calculate how I missed doing something she asked me to do. I'm literally dumbfounded. I'm pretty sure she didn't actually tell me she wanted me to stop at any antique store, but if she says she did, maybe she did. I'm wrong more often than not about things like this. At least, I always seem to be the one apologizing. And besides, I don't even remember the conversation all that well.

But by now, concerns about whether we'll get back in time to watch the football game on television have started crowding into my mind, so I just mutter, "Sorry." Then I spend the rest of the day trying to make up for it.

I'll do almost anything my wife asks me to do, but she has to ask in a way I'll understand. I don't take hints well, and I certainly can't read her mind. After twenty-three years of marriage, I'm beginning to catch on to this female riddle-talk. But now, with a teenage daughter trying to perfect it as well, I'm confused all over again.

Moms, speak plainly to your boys. You'll save all of us a lot of headaches. Say what you mean, and mean what you say.

## Touch, Eye Contact, and Sound Bites

A boy's mind is easily distracted. He does, however, react well to visual stimulation, noise, and physical contact—the old hunting traits. So try the touch-sight-sound approach to get his attention.

First, remove distractions from his line of vision. Turn off the television or at least mute the sound. Contrary to what we may say, men (and boys) are not capable of reading the newspaper and listening to you at the same time. Our brains are not wired to be able to do several things at once. It's why we can focus with fierce intensity and accomplish great things, but our multitasking skills suffer for it. My wife might be able to watch television, talk on the phone, bandage a kid's wound, and cook dinner all at the same time, but I can't.

Second, touch your boy to get his attention. Gently put a hand on his elbow or shoulder. As soon as he looks at you, make eye contact with him. Feel free to use a variety of facial expressions. Remember, boys are very visual, so a memorable look from you might make a big impact. In fact, I encourage you to develop a look. My son, at an early age, started getting a little edgy whenever Dad was giving him "the look."

I remember one of my eighth-grade teachers. Her name was Ms. See, and she taught Science Fiction, a reading class. She was quite attractive, but she had a laser-beam glare that could shut down the most smart-aleck delinquent in a matter of seconds. We used to joke that we could feel her look boring into the back of our heads like a drill without even seeing her. She never had to yell or raise her voice. She'd just give us the look for about ten seconds, and we'd slink off to a corner to hide. Nobody disrespected Ms. See.

Third, speak succinctly in small, sound-bite-size sentences. Keep your comments short and to the point, such as, "Don't do that anymore," or "Why? Because men don't act that way."

My wife tends to give our kids long lectures. She feels that's her duty. Maybe so, but after about sixty seconds of lecturing, I can see the kids' eyes starting to glaze over. After two minutes *my* head starts nodding. Eventually, she's angry because the kids aren't listening, the kids are resentful because they're always getting lectured, and I'm just trying to keep the peace. Lectures have their place. But they're like triple-fudge chocolate ice cream—a little bit goes a long way. Constant long-ranging conversations are difficult for a boy to track. But periodic well-chosen conversations will likely give him a more relaxed attitude about coming to you.

Keep in mind the age of your son and the appropriateness of your communication style. For instance, lecturing a three-year-old on the dangers of touching a hot stove would not be very effective. A tersely said "No!" would be a more effective form of communicating that message. As boys get older, life experience stories seem to work better than lectures. Also, asking a boy what he thinks about a subject is a good way to get him talking about an issue.

Communicate that you are always there for your son. Then respect his communications as privileged. I've never felt more betrayed than when I've spoken to my wife (or my mother when I was younger) about a sensitive, heartfelt subject, only to find that she had discussed it with one of her friends. Women process information by discussing it with other women, but males feel this is a breach of confidentiality. This can be particularly disturbing to a young man trying to develop a trusting relationship, especially in a single-parent situation.

Try speaking softly sometimes. Often you have to yell at boys to get through to them, but sometimes changing the volume or tone of your voice works wonders. Whisper; it sparks their curiosity.

Finally, have him repeat what you said and ask if he understands. That's all there is to it. There's an old acronym used for putting information into computers—KISS stands for Keep It Simple, Stupid, meaning the less complicated the message that goes in, the less chance it will become messed up coming out. Boys are like computers. The less complicated the data they have to process, the better.

For years, the Portland Trail Blazers professional basketball team employed a radio and television announcer, an icon named Bill Schonley. Schonley had a special saying for a quick slam-dunk-type play: "Bingo, bango, bongo—lickety brindle down the middle!" That's how best to communicate a message to your son—bingo, bango, bongo! Short, sweet, and to the point. If you feel the need for lengthy conversation, you should probably call up a girlfriend—it'll be a lot more satisfying for both you and your son.

Taking these approaches to communicating with your boy may initially require a little more effort, but it's easier than having to yell at him four or five times, threaten him, punish him, and in the end finally ruin your day too.

## Reinforce with Activity

If you want to talk to your son (or any male in your life, for that matter), try talking to him while doing something he enjoys. Four words strike fear into every male's heart: "We need to talk." Men *can* talk; we just don't *like* to. When I hear those words, I instantly start thinking of what I could possibly have done wrong and searching for excuses why I did it. Those words usually signify a problem to a man, and men only talk about problems when they mean to blame someone or ask for advice. They don't solve problems by talking about them. If a woman is really upset, a man assumes she's blaming him for something.[4]

Frank Pittman says it this way in his book *Man Enough*:

> Men hear anything a woman says with strong emotion as just hysterical carrying-on. And while a woman's anger is as terrifying to a man as the wrath of an angry god, we don't hear what a woman says when she's angry; we only hear that she is angry and we strap ourselves in, turn off our receivers, and wait in terror for the storm to pass. When we men have any important message to deliver, we deliver it as logically and unemotionally as possible. We know that what we say when we're angry should be

> ignored, and our friends do us the favor of ignoring it. We often wish women would do the same.[5]

Males are at a disadvantage in conversations, because females generally have better language skills. I used to resent the fact that my wife could manipulate conversations to her advantage due to her superior communication skills. Naturally, this meant I was guaranteed to lose any argument we entered into, whether I was wrong or not (of course, I was always wrong). In my frustration, I would tell her, "Just because I can't express myself adequately doesn't mean I'm wrong." I find it interesting that most men take it for granted that they will be the ones apologizing for any disagreement they have with their wives. That's probably not a good way to start a conversation.

As a casual observer, I've watched on a number of occasions mothers and their sons in heated discussions about one thing or another. Often, the mother, with her superior verbal skills, is capable of dominating the conversation. Frequently, the frustrated boy ends up resorting to anger to make himself understood. The Bible exhorts fathers not to exasperate or discourage their children. The same applies to mothers.

On the other hand, I've witnessed mothers use their communication proficiency to help their sons express themselves beautifully. I saw one mother skillfully and patiently draw out her son's thoughts, helping him realize emotions he wasn't even aware he was feeling, all the while building him up and making him feel good about their relationship. It was quite inspiring to see her using her gifts for such a good cause.

I confess that I dread having those "meaningful" discussions with my wife on the confines of the couch. It's like being shackled in a dungeon. I can almost hear the oppressive dirge music playing. But let her take me golfing or hiking, and I'll talk to her all day long! What is more, I'll talk about what she wants to talk about. And, I admit, I'll probably be more receptive to her concerns.

The same thing applies to boys. Take your son somewhere fun and talk to him during the activity. Shoot some hoops or take him someplace special. If you can't shoot a basketball, just catch it and throw it to him while he shoots. Take him to the carnival. Be sure to let him win a prize for you at the target-shooting game. Take him in the woods to collect bugs or frogs. You don't have to handle the critters, but just being there signifies to him that you care. Also, a positive memory of a good time will reinforce whatever you talk to him about.

Why does this approach work? I suspect doing something the boy enjoys takes the pressure off having to think and talk at the same time. This may not make sense, but I don't know of any other way to explain it. Maybe it removes the emotions from the discussion, creating an easier environment for males to express themselves. Having a physical outlet makes males more comfortable than making eye contact. This is a lifelong attribute of males. The other day I was being interviewed by a case worker for the Big Brothers Big Sisters organization in preparation of becoming a big brother for a young fatherless boy. After an hour of conversation, she asked how I would best communicate with a boy. I stated, "We would do something physical. Just having sat here and talked for an hour has me jumping out of my skin! I feel like getting up and pacing around the room." The tension I was feeling was literally palpable—it was all I could do just to sit still!

Males need to move, especially when they are upset or when they are problem solving. They also need to think about their feelings before they can express them, unlike women who can think, feel, and talk all at the same time.[6] Performing a physical activity allows them to think before having to answer.

This might appear to contradict the idea of removing distractions before speaking to boys, but this tactic applies to situations where a longer discussion is required—times when more than sound-bite-size sentences are needed. This might be a good technique to save for lecture-size topics. Also, presenting lectures in a problem-solving format can make it easier for your son to take ownership of the discussion. Males instinctively try to solve problems. Say something like, "We have a problem, and I was wondering if I could get your help in solving it."

Here's another tip. The best places to take boys are (1) a gravel pit, (2) a construction site, or (3) the dump. Men know this—women don't. Here's why these places rank high on a boy's list of activities.

Gravel pits are just plain cool! You can find all sorts of treasures, such as rocks, arrowheads, old bottles, or fossils. If you take your son to a gravel pit, let him collect and bring home plenty of cool rocks! So what if his room is filled with rocks, dead (or live) bugs, and animal skeletons? It's just a room.

Construction sites have big, powerful pieces of machinery and heavy equipment. They're loud and dirty and filled

**Strategies for Conversing with Boys**

1. Make a point in one or two sentences, not much more.
2. Tell a story or anecdote to illustrate the point.
3. Ask for a response. If none is forthcoming, try asking for a story. "Is there a time you did something like that?"
4. Listen for the key word or words in the response. These words usually will involve primary feelings, either in direct language or by reference—*afraid*, *hurt*, *Wow!*
5. Use those key words as your entrance to the continuing conversation. "What were you afraid of?"
6. Don't be afraid to allow silences in the conversation. Sometimes boys need time to think or process.
7. As conversation deepens, it's often useful to be doing something together, not just sitting across the table trying for eye-to-eye emotive intensity.
8. As much as possible, end conversations with an invitation for the boy to have the last word. Let him end the conversation.
9. Bring it up again in some other way as needed. So often, boys don't "get it" just one time around.[7]

with sweaty, burly men. Boys (and men) stand with their mouths open in awe for hours, watching the goings-on.

I'm not sure what the fascination with the dump is all about. It may have something to do with ritual male bonding. My son speaks in reverent tones about our past trips to the dump. In fact, I still like to go to the dump with my dad. Maybe it's just because they're dirty and smelly and there are no women around. I do know that my son, even as a teenager, will jump at the chance to go to the dump. Besides, the best stories always happen at the dump. Like the time when my brother and I were seven and eleven years old and a seagull "bombed" my stepfather's forehead. That's still a good story to tell around the kitchen table when we get together.

## Admiration and Respect

Men and boys typically require admiration and respect even more than they do love. Does that surprise you? As a man, I like being loved, but what I really crave from my wife and children (especially my wife) is respect and admiration.

In twenty-three years of marriage, I can vividly remember two things my wife, Suzanne, has said to me. Once, after we had both read an action-adventure novel where the protagonist overcame great odds, she said the hero reminded her of me. Wow! I don't think she thought much about it, but to me it was like she was showering me with love—she admired me! And, at least by my interpretation of her comments, she considered me a hero. I believed the story's hero to be a man's man—competent, strong, tough, and able to solve any problem through action and perseverance.

The second thing she said occurred about three years ago. I was asked to go on stage at our church with my family and give my testimony during each of eight Easter weekend services. After it was all over, Suzanne and I were talking about our weekend's experiences. Suzanne offhandedly said, "I'm so proud of you. All those other women in church were looking at me and wishing it was their husband on stage." I know she didn't understand the power of that statement. But the catch in her voice conveyed her excitement to me. I was ready to climb the

Empire State Building for her. She could have asked me for anything at that moment, and I would have killed myself trying to get it for her. My wife was proud of me.

All males, big and little, want the women (including moms) in their lives to be proud of them. We enjoy impressing our ladies. When I think about it, most of my life's accomplishments have come about, either directly or indirectly, as a result of trying to earn my wife's praise and approval. It's not always a conscious decision, but the desire for her respect and admiration is always in the back of my mind. There's nothing I want more than for my wife to be proud of me. I suspect most males are motivated in a similar fashion. Your son wants you to be proud of him and is motivated by that desire. Would you like to reinforce a positive behavior in your son, or even change a negative one? When your son does something you want to encourage, try saying something like, "I really admire the fact that you did that," or "I respect you for that. That's how a man acts." Or if you see another man exhibit a behavior you want your son to emulate, try saying, "I really respect that quality in a man. That's how a real man acts." Watch your son's chest swell when you build him up with the qualities of admiration and respect. And when he warrants it, be sure to tell him that you're proud of him. He will do his best to try to get that response from you again.

Cooking your son's favorite meal as a reward also works wonders as positive reinforcement. Yes, I know, it sounds too simple, but it works. We males really aren't as complicated as you might think.

Likewise, to change a negative behavior, try saying, "Oh, I'm so disappointed in your behavior. I've never thought a man would act that way." He might not like it, but he'll be thinking about it. Start talking to your son this way from an early age. Give him a standard to work toward. Boys like to know the rules (mainly so they know what they can get away with).

Remember, though, males tend to view criticism not as an opportunity to learn and grow but as an attack on their adequacy or even their masculinity. Many men and boys are convinced that to be criticized implies an admission of failure, inadequacy, or incompetence.[8] Also, I'm sure you've noticed the reaction you get from your son when he feels like he's needed. Consider times when you've said something like, "Can you open this pickle jar for me?" or "Could you reach that plate for me?" They usually come strutting over and gladly handle the task Mom needs done—especially little guys. They'll come running to help Mom do something she can't do for herself. Males are motivated and empowered when they feel needed.

Communicating with boys is not easy. However, women, with their superior verbal and intuitive abilities, can generally find a way to penetrate some of the genetic traits that hinder a male's ability to listen, understand, and communicate. We may not always say it, but we always appreciate it when you do.

## Questions for Discussion

1. Describe a time when you felt like you were speaking to a brick wall when you talked to your son.
2. What tips have you learned in this chapter that would make communicating with your son easier?
3. Where can you take your son to talk so he can have fun at the same time?

# 6

# Disciplining Boys

> Correct your son, and he will give you rest;
> Yes, he will give delight to your soul.
>
> *Proverbs 29:17*

When disciplining boys, especially teenagers, my advice is to pick your battles. There will be many battles, and you can't fight them all. Well, you can—you just won't win them all. Know the values that are most important to you, and impart those to your son. Draw the battle lines on the important issues, and you'll have a better chance of succeeding than if you make a big production over everything. Let the small stuff slide. Part of your son growing into a man is making decisions on his own, suffering because of the choices he's made, and learning from his mistakes. Especially as he gets older, your role is to guide rather than lecture or make every decision for him. This allows him to develop the leadership skills he will need as a man.

## Consequences and Accountability

Boys need structure and supervision. They need to be "civilized." They can be civilized, in part, by knowing what the rules are. Males are uncomfortable when they find themselves in situations with ambiguous rules. I remember as a boy making a game out of virtually everything, even doing chores. If I succeeded by the rules I invented or the rules already in place, I attained much satisfaction. Boys like to compete and win. It's hard to compete when there are no rules or when the rules keep changing. And without rules, there are no standards by which to be held accountable. Establish rules for your son early in his development, ones where he is accountable to someone other than himself. Then enforce them.

When teaching your son to be accountable, you need to be clear about your expectations. Establish concrete consequences for not following through on those expectations. That's how he learns responsibility. But be sure to be specific on what you want done. A teen especially takes advantage of anything that's vague or unspecified. That leaves room for him to complete your request when and how he wants to. Most likely, his concept of when and how is different from yours. Why do males need to be accountable to someone other than themselves? Why do boys need to be trained in this character trait that is rapidly becoming lost within our culture?

Dennis Rainey of FamilyLife talks about the characteristics of the unaccountable. He once sat down and wrote a list of characteristics of people who have fallen to temptation. Over and over, this was how other people described them:

- has a loose spirit with few boundaries
- rationalizes and justifies behavior
- is detached, reclusive, insulated from people
- makes decisions without consulting others
- has a lack of authenticity and realness about his or her life
- is defensive, proud, unwilling to admit mistakes and failures
- hides major areas of life from others
- is intimidating, unapproachable, secretive

Rainey says, "It's amazing to see how these descriptions pop up again and again. They [the unaccountable] are isolated, keeping people at arm's length, and not willing to submit themselves to the scrutiny of others. When you are isolated, you are much more susceptible to temptation."[1]

Allowing people into our lives is an important factor in maintaining accountability—a skill in which boys and men need to be trained. Accountability helps males keep from falling into temptation with soul killers such as drugs, alcohol abuse, gambling, pornography, and adultery.

So temptation, which we know destroys families, is one reason men and boys need accountability in their lives. Another reason is developing character. It's been my experience that many talented young people need to be accountable to someone who will push them to exert the effort required to achieve their best. For this reason, involving your son in an organized sport could provide him with both a character-building training ground and an accountability partner—in the person of the coach.

A coach's job description has traditionally been to get more effort and talent out of his players than they are capable of extracting from themselves. Additionally, a coach's goal is to teach boys character traits such as hard work, respect, self-discipline, and teamwork.

Unfortunately, mothers, with their innate desire to protect their children and their children's feelings, sometimes sabotage the accountability process without meaning to. Consider, for example, the "mean old coach" scenario: In an effort to teach Johnny respect or self-discipline, his high school coach either takes away his starting position, limits his playing time, or verbally challenges him in front of the team to improve his performance and practice habits. Little Johnny, upon being subjected to what he perceives as unfair treatment, runs home to Mommy (I never seem to read about Dad being involved in any of these situations), crying about how the mean old coach abused him. Mommy is aghast and immediately charges down to complain to the school superintendent. This all too often results in the coach getting fired (sometimes without even getting to tell his side of the story), followed by the coach appealing to the local school board for justice. The board, more often concerned with funding and public relations than finding the truth, usually backs the superintendent's decision.

This seems to be happening with ever-increasing regularity. During the recent firing of a local high school boys' baseball coach for allegedly mistreating his players, one school board member stated, "I think we are confusing teaching discipline and respect with something else." Ironically, the board voted unanimously that the coach did not verbally or physically abuse anyone on the team but still upheld the superintendent's decision to fire him.

There are certainly some bad coaches who are abusive and deserve to be fired. But the vast majority of coaches are dedicated, hardworking individuals who are just trying to better the kids they work with through the principles of sports. Today, however, in our culture of instant gratification and relative truth, coaches (from the pros right down through high school) seem to have been relegated to the roles of psychologist, babysitter, and self-esteem counselor. Unfortunately, now they have to spend all their time worrying about whether everyone plays exactly the same amount and whether anyone's feelings get hurt.

By running too quickly to rescue their sons when things get tough, some moms are teaching their boys that the way out of hard times is to find someone (a woman) to get them off the hook rather than to be accountable to the one in authority and step up to the plate. This can set patterns for boys' entire lives. A boy who avoids accountability becomes a man who is answerable to no one—a recipe for disaster. You may also be training him to base his decision-making skills on feelings instead of principles. I'll trust a man who uses principles to make decisions over one who uses emotions every time. Emotions are unreliable and subject to change on a whim. Principles are like lighthouses that guide ships away from treacherous rocks that would tear holes in their hulls, sinking them and killing all aboard.

After reading the "mean old coach" scenario, a female friend of mine raised the following questions: "So if I've been in an abusive relationship, how do I know how tough is tough enough and what is too tough? How do I resist trying to save my son from the kind of situation that was hard and painful for me?" These are excellent questions. My first suggestion is that if you think your son is being mistreated by a coach or other authority figure, ask a man you trust for his thoughts on the situation. Often a man can give you an objective opinion on what constitutes masculine discipline as opposed to abuse. Then if you are still concerned about your son's treatment by a coach, you should first approach the coach directly. If for some reason you are uncomfortable with that, perhaps parents of other players have similar concerns and you could approach the coach as a group. If you don't get a satisfactory response to your concerns from the coach, *then* take it to the athletic director, principal, and administrative personnel—in that order. Approach upper levels of administration in any organization as a last resort, not as your first response. Every organization has a chain of command. Your example of following the appropriate levels in that chain of command also teaches your son the importance of following the rules of our society.

Coaches are not the only male authority figures who should hold boys accountable for their behavior. It's equally important for other males, even indirectly or

## Behavior Management Using Consequences

There are generally two types of consequences: reinforcement and punishment. Although reinforcement is generally more effective and should be used more often, punishment may also be used in an effective program of behavior management. Following are several types of punishment.

**Restricting Privileges**

Restricting privileges is an effective means of punishment. This technique will vary according to the age and preferences of the child. For example, taking telephone or car privileges from a teen might be very effective. Similarly, restricting access to the television, video games, a bicycle, or other favorite toy might be more effective for an elementary-school-age child.

**Time-Out**

A punishment technique commonly used with preschool-age children is time-out. In order to use time-out effectively, adults must realize that it creates an unpleasant situation for children because it provides time *away* from anything reinforcing, such as toys, other children, or adults. If adults are talking to a child while he is in time-out, the adults' attention is actually rewarding the child! Similarly, sending a child to his room for time-out is rewarding, because he has access to all his toys. To maximize the effectiveness of this procedure, select a location that is removed from family activity and other interesting items. A chair facing a blank wall works well. In addition, remember that attention is reinforcing, so adults must not interact with the child during the time-out period.

**Graded Consequences**

Often, using graded consequences that increase in severity is effective in reducing unwanted behaviors. For example, a child may lose video game privileges for one day the first time an unwanted behavior occurs. The second time the behavior occurs, the child might be grounded for one day, and so on.

Adults must clearly define consequences before children's behavior occurs. Consistency is crucial in this process. Remember, rewards are more effective than punishments, and adult attention is very rewarding to children. Thus, adults should spend more time and attention on desired behaviors than undesired behaviors.[2]

as a consequence of coming in contact with them during the course of life, to hold boys accountable for their actions.

My son and I try to go on wilderness camping trips each summer. We pack up whatever we can carry on our backs and hike into a remote area of wilderness for four or five days, living off the land and whatever fish we can catch. We carry some freeze-dried food just in case. Several years ago we went to the Strawberry Mountain Wilderness area in eastern Oregon. On the way home, we took a detour and stopped at the tiny town of Fossil, Oregon, to dig up some fossils on the side of the hill above the high school football field. Later we stopped at the only ice cream parlor/casket shop west of the Mississippi. As we sat drinking a delicious milkshake, an interesting event took place.

Several tables over from ours sat two local teenage girls, a baby, and a scruffy-looking young man who was evidently dating one of the girls. After several minutes a giant of a man walked in with his two little girls. It was clear that the big man knew the teenage girls, as they introduced him to the young man accompanying them. As if suspecting what was to come, the young ladies scurried off to the ice cream counter with the baby and the man's little girls. The big man reached out and said hello, engulfing the younger man's hand in his giant paw. Much to the younger male's surprise, he didn't let go of his hand as their discussion continued. I smiled as I overheard their discussion. While I couldn't hear the younger man's responses, he visibly became more and more uncomfortable as the following discussion ensued:

Big guy: "What's your name, son?"

Young fellow: Mumble, mumble.

BG: "What school do you go to? Where do you live?"

YF: Mutter, mumble—mutter.

BG: "What's your daddy's name?"

YF: Mumble, squeak.

BG: "Your family the Smith people over near the town of John Day?"

YF: Hsmnt.

BG: "I know your daddy—he's a good man. Son, nice meetin' ya. Y'all have fun and treat these girls right now."

He let go of the young man's hand and walked off to the ice cream counter as the young man nearly crumbled in relief. The big guy had effectively told this young man, "I know who you are, I know where to find you, and I know your family. If anything happens to these girls, you'll be accountable to me." That's how men hold younger men accountable for their actions. I guarantee you, that young man will think twice before doing something irresponsible with those young ladies. That big man had no vested interest in protecting those girls except the responsibility every man has to look after and protect women. Also, I suspect he will want another man to look after his daughters that way when they get older. Unfortunately, this type of manly accountability probably happens only in small rural communities anymore—if at all.

Women also play an important role in holding boys accountable for their behavior. I remember when I was about twelve years old. At that time long hair was cool. I had very long hair, so I was very "cool." My little brother had always been forced by my parents to wear his hair in a crew cut. I continually teased him over the years, calling him "skinhead" and "baldy." And of course, it produced the desired result of sending him crying to Mom. One day, after repeated warnings to cease my teasing, my mother cornered me on the front porch, took an electric razor, and shaved my beautiful locks down to the scalp. I'm not sure if that action was an example of a healthy child rearing technique or not, but I certainly never again called my brother names after that—at least not within hearing of my mother.

Males must be accountable to someone other than themselves, be it to their wives, other men, their mothers, their fathers, or God—their heavenly Father. Without that accountability, they tend to make their own rules or codes of conduct, and that spells trouble (evidenced by what happens in the book *Lord of the Flies*). Boys need to learn from an early age to be accountable and to understand that their actions have either positive or negative consequences.

## Challenging Authority

> A child that is allowed to be disrespectful to his parents will not have true respect for anyone.
>
> Author unknown

Boys have a natural tendency to challenge authority. It's part of developing the leadership skills they will need later in life. However, they need to learn when it's appropriate to lead and when it's appropriate to follow. Single moms

### Wanda's Story

Wanda and her husband could not have children, so they decided to adopt. They adopted three biracial baby boys, two of whom were brothers. Soon after adopting, Wanda became pregnant with a son. Within three years, Wanda's husband decided he didn't want to be a husband or a father after all. He left Wanda a single mother with four boys to raise by herself. Times were tough over the next ten years.

Wanda says the biggest problem she faced was lack of money. "Trying to feed four boys was a real chore. But I'm glad I didn't have girls," she says with a laugh. "They require more clothes and other expensive things that boys don't need."

Wanda says her boys were very loyal to her. They never complained about the lack of money and even got jobs to help out as soon as they were old enough.

When one of her sons was accepted to play football in a private league, Wanda didn't have the money. A pastor from a local church offered to donate the fee, but she turned him down. "I had foolish pride. I said, 'We don't accept charity.'" Eventually she accepted his offer, which led to her and the boys attending that church.

Wanda's boys are all in their mid- to late twenties now. Three are successful professionals, but one suffers from a drug abuse problem. She gives the following advice to single moms raising boys:

1) "You've got to have a firm hold on boys. They are rambunctious, high-spirited, and active. Know what they are doing at all times. Always question who, what, and where whenever they are going somewhere."
2) "Don't back down. I've always told them I'm raising men, not boys."
3) "Don't just threaten—follow through. So be very careful what you say."
4) "Get to know each child's personality."

especially need to lead their families with authority. Mothers often do not have the assumed position of authority that fathers have in the family. Nor do they instill the fear factor in their children that fathers seem to possess.

If you're a single mom, don't allow guilt over your situation to make you overly permissive. Punish your children when it's needed, hug them when they need assurance, and make them think you know what you're doing even when you don't have a clue. Part of maintaining control in a leadership position is to not be undecided, passive, or hesitant even in uncertain situations. That's not to say that a leader should be domineering, but your boy needs to know you are in control, not him. He will quickly seize the opportunity to usurp your authority if you waver in your command. I've never seen an army general exhibit indecisiveness or uncertainty when making decisions. You are the general of your little army, at least until your children are old enough to participate in decision making. Make your decisions and stick with them. If you're wrong, admit it, ask for forgiveness, and move on.

Body language is very important for asserting authority. Most high school football coaches are shorter than their players. Next time you're watching practice, notice that they make the team "take a knee" when they speak to them. That's so the boys are looking up at the coach instead of vice versa. Make your six-foot-two-inch teenage son take a knee or sit when you talk to him so that you are at least eye level instead of looking up at him from a subservient position.

Also, a little unpredictability in a woman is scary to a male. When my huge son, Frank, scurries by and whispers,

"Mom's crazy," with a tremor in his voice, I instinctively know what he's talking about. Mom's on the warpath about something, and we both know it's time to find somewhere to hide for a while until the storm passes. Frank might be a foot taller and a hundred pounds heavier than his mother, but he's convinced she's capable of doing just about anything, and that keeps him in line.

Sometimes young men can be quite lazy, neglecting responsibilities or being downright disagreeable. When openly defiant behavior raises its ugly head, the best response allows you to be really tough and nice at the same time. Instead of yelling or pounding the table, just say in a calm voice, "You'll wish you hadn't." Then let it go . . . for the time being. In the next few days or weeks, your son will come to you with requests for money, a ride, the car keys, etc. That's the "day of reckoning," when you gently and briefly remind him, "Remember the other day when I told you, 'You'll wish you hadn't'? Well, that time has come." It'll be a tough moment for him—and you—but it's a great opportunity for your son to learn how life really works.

## Anger Control

> We're not always aware of subliminal messages we send, like "Big boys don't cry" or "Stop whining," which is a reflection of society's credo that men should not show their emotions. Boys and men are not inherently less emotional than women; they are taught to be that way, which means that mothers and fathers have an important responsibility in raising sons who are aware of their emotions.
>
> Elyse Zorn Karlin, *Sons: A Mother's Manual*

Anger is a God-given emotion. Only love is mentioned more frequently in the Bible. However, anger is a secondary emotion often used to mask other emotions.

Gary and Carrie Oliver say this about anger in males:

> Anger is often the only emotion that a male is aware of, though they've surely experienced a myriad of other emotions as well. For just below the surface, a man has many other, deeper emotions that need to be identified and acknowledged. Hidden underneath (sometimes deep underneath) the surface emotion of anger is fear, hurt, frustration, disappointment, vulnerability, and longing for connection. Boys learn early on that anger can help them deflect attention from these more painful emotions. Anger is safer, and it provides some protection for the frightened and vulnerable self. Anger helps him avoid, or at least minimize, his pain. Anger provides a surge of energy. It decreases his vulnerability and increases his sense of security. What's more, he tells himself, all real men get angry. In short, boys learn quickly that it's easier to feel anger than it is to feel pain.[3]

Having been raised in an alcoholic home, I was brought up in a culture steeped in fear—fear of everything from not knowing whether the ambulance would come to our house that night to never knowing what reaction even an innocent facial expression might provoke. A loud noise was guaranteed to provoke an angry reaction from a parent with a hangover. Because of that, sudden, loud noises provoke a fearful (angry) reaction from me to this day. As a child, I felt like the ground was never steady under my feet and the rug might get jerked out from under me at any moment.

As a very young man, I one day came to the realization that anger conquered fear. If I just got mad, I never had to face the humiliating emotion of fear again. After I attained a certain physical size, my anger protected me, my brothers and sisters, and even my mother from physical abuse. I remember saying to myself, "Never again will I be afraid of anything or anybody." Of course, that was ridiculous. I spent a majority of my adult life being afraid of many things; I just covered it by being angry. Unfortunately, fear is a lonely companion. But I clearly remember the moment when I understood the power of anger and how it kept me from being so scared.

Anger can, however, be used productively if channeled properly. When I first started my company, I pitched my wares to as many potential clients as possible. I met with a local bank vice president in charge of environmental affairs. He sat and stared at me for half an hour as I laid myself bare, offering up my services and qualifications. Finally he stopped me and said viciously, completely out of the blue, "You'll never make it. You're just another mom-and-pop fraud hanging out their shingle. If I have anything to say, you'll never work in this town." Shocked, I felt as if I'd been attacked for no apparent reason. I crawled out of his office with my tail between my legs and felt sorry for myself for about two days. Then I got mad. "Who does he think he is, anyway? I'll show him who's a fraud!" Using this motivation, I vowed to succeed no matter what.

I never did find out why he despised me so. Fifteen years later, he's no longer around, but I'm still in business and doing well. I used my anger toward him as motivation to succeed. Whenever I didn't feel like doing something, I'd think about that incident, and all of a sudden

I'd find myself doing all the little, unpleasant tasks it took to prevail.

Uncontrolled anger in males often leads to violent behavior. Boys have always committed more acts of violence than girls. However, it appears that this violence has escalated over the past several years—particularly, although not exclusively, in neighborhoods where fathers are absent (physically or emotionally) to a higher degree. The inability of young men to control their anger is one reason mentioned for this increase in violence among our youth.

Mary Kay Blakely, in *American Mom*, says, "It takes twenty or so years before a mother can know with any certainty how effective her theories have been—and even then there are surprises. The daily newspapers raise the most frightening questions of all for a mother of sons: Could my once sweet babes ever become violent men? Are my sons really who I think they are?"[4]

Anger is a destructive emotion. It seems that the greater your love for someone, the greater your capacity to experience a wide range of emotions toward him or her—*including* the harmful emotions of irritation, resentment, anger, and rage.[5]

Single moms, if your son acts out his anger often or inappropriately, especially at you, there could be some very logical explanations. Your son has had his worst fears in life come true—the loss of his dad and the breakup of his family, all of which were beyond his control. If he exhibits anger, he very likely is using it to mask emotions such as fear, hurt, frustration, and disappointment. His anger at you could also be a form of displacement, which is what happens when he's mad at someone or something and then dumps his anger on an innocent party such as yourself. It's important that you teach him that anger is a secondary emotion that covers another emotion. Help him discover what he is really feeling so that in the future he learns to control and understand this potentially destructive emotion.

If your son is angry much of the time, is depressed, or exhibits characteristics such as continuously fighting or picking on smaller children or animals, you may want to seek professional help.

## Teach Them to Work

> A man at work, making something which he feels will exist because he is working at it and wills it, is exercising the energies of his mind and soul as well as of his body. Memory and imagination help him as he works. Not only his own thoughts, but the thoughts of the men of past ages guide his hands; and, as part of the human race, he creates. If we work thus we shall be men, and our days will be happy and eventful.
>
> William Morris

One of the basic tenets of manhood is work. Males need to work; it's part of our makeup. Work gives us a sense of fulfillment and achievement—it gives us a positive self-esteem. When business is brisk and I'm working hard, I feel good about myself. When business is slow, I don't—I feel useless. It's not that what I do distinguishes who I am so much as that when I'm working and providing for my family, I feel more manly. Boys also need the positive self-image that comes from tackling a project and completing it with the sweat of their brows.

Work gives meaning to men's lives. Joseph Conrad said in *Heart of Darkness*, "I don't like work—no man does—but I like what is in work—the chance to find yourself. Your own reality—for yourself, not for others—what no man can ever know."[6]

Give boys chores at an early age. It keeps them busy and teaches them both work ethic and responsibility. It also engages them and gives them a feeling of ownership toward the family and the household. Boys who don't learn that taking care of chores around the house is part of their contribution to the family often end up expecting the women in their lives to serve them. A female friend of mine recently said, "How is it that some men seem to grow up and expect their wives to wait on them? Because Mom did? Moms don't do their future daughters-in-law a favor by picking up after junior." Well said.

Teach your son to budget money by giving him a small allowance starting at a young age. He'll need budgeting skills when he has a family. If you can't afford an allowance, cook your son's favorite meal as payment for his work. Males—big or small—love to have their favorite food prepared for them as a reward. It's not the money that really matters. It's the concept of a day's wages for a day's work.

When you do something special for your son—like cook his favorite meal—let him know it's because you appreciate all the work he's done. Many times males don't recognize the cause-benefit relationship if it is not brought to their attention. For instance, I try to give my

**Age-Appropriate Chores**

| | |
|---|---|
| Ages 2–3 | Hang up clothes on hook<br>Help pick up toys<br>Help feed pets |
| Ages 4–5 | Make own bed<br>Set table and clear dishes from table<br>Dust furniture<br>Help put groceries away |
| Ages 6–12 | Take care of pets<br>Cook simple foods<br>Help wash car<br>Vacuum, sweep, mop<br>Clean bathroom<br>Do laundry<br>Take out trash |
| Ages 13 and up | Wash windows<br>Clean stove and oven<br>Prepare meal<br>Mow lawn[7] |

wife "just 'cuz" flowers every now and again—just 'cuz I haven't given her any lately, and just 'cuz I love her. Inevitably, she cooks a meal I enjoy shortly thereafter. Chances are that I will have forgotten by that time that I gave her flowers and I won't make the connection that she is doing something nice for me because I did something nice for her.

Give your son a vision for "conquering" his own house, especially the "manly" things, such as completing yard projects, helping the fix-it man, or maybe even painting something. You'll find that he'll be much happier and more satisfied and content with the man he's becoming.

## Questions for Discussion

1. How do you discipline your son? What ways can you think of to teach him accountability for his actions? Talk to your group of women about why boys need to understand consequences.
2. When would be a good time to have discussions with your son about anger? (Hint: not when he's angry.) What problems has males' anger caused in your family?
3. Establish a set of weekly chores for your son. Discuss with him why chores are important and what rewards he will receive for fulfilling his responsibility. (Note: Rewards don't have to be monetary.)

# 7

# What Do Boys Need to Learn to Become Good Men?

God give us men! A time like this demands
Strong minds, great hearts, true faith, and ready hands;
Men whom the lust of office does not kill;
Men whom the spoils of office cannot buy;
Men who possess opinions and a will;
Men who have honor; men who will not lie.

*Josiah Gilbert Holland,* Wanted

## What Is a Man?

When we say someone's name, our minds instantly picture that person. Different character traits that embody that individual come to mind. When you think of what makes a good man, what character traits come to mind? Here's what I think a good man is all about. I still get goose bumps when I remember this incident.

On the Friday following the 9/11 terrorist attack against our country, I was scheduled to have lunch with my good friend Jim. Jim is the pastor of a small start-up church here in Oregon. As we stood in line to order our food, Jim leaned over and whispered, "I'm going to pray out loud at noon like President Bush requested." Jim was really nervous and asked if I had any suggestions on how to go about this. I responded somewhat tritely, but truthfully, "Nope. Better you than me."

As the noon hour approached, Jim stood up and said in a loud voice to the entire restaurant, "Could I have your attention, please? President Bush has asked the nation to pray for our country at noon today. I don't want to offend anyone, but we're going to be praying at our table, and I'd like to invite you to join us if you want."

A stunned silence greeted Jim's speech. Frankly, I admit, I was a little embarrassed. Jim sat down, and as we waited the five minutes for noon to arrive, no one came over. Just before we began to pray, a woman approached with her young son in tow and asked, "Could we join you? I think what you are doing is great."

At the appointed time, Jim began to pray out loud. With my head bowed, I heard the scraping of one or two other people pulling up chairs around our table. Jim prayed out loud for our country, our president and other leaders, our military personnel, and the families of the victims of 9/11. He prayed passionately from his heart. I estimate he prayed for about twenty minutes. During the whole time, I did not hear any talking, music, or even doors opening and closing.

As he finished, I opened my eyes and looked around. What I saw astounded me. The entire restaurant—perhaps twenty-five people, including the cooks and servers—were gathered around our table. Many had tears in their eyes. An entire restaurant had closed its operations during its busiest time of day. The owner came over with tears in her eyes and thanked us, saying, "You can pray here any time you'd like."

Everyone had stopped what they were doing and had come over to pray, all because of the courage and leadership of one man. It was quite literally one of the manliest displays I've ever seen. Now whenever I say or hear Jim's name, this example of his leadership and courage always comes to mind. I'm especially pleased that the young mother who first joined us brought her son. She showed much courage by being the first one to break the silence with action, thereby freeing up everyone else to act as well. Her son was blessed to have witnessed the courage displayed by both his mother and Jim.

There's a school of thought that encourages us to "speak it into existence." For instance, when you tell a man he's brave, you help him become brave. With that in mind, tell your son all the things you want him to be: courageous, loyal, honest, strong, tender, and compassionate. Remind him of these qualities, and you help instill them within him. Point them out in others so he can see them in action. When you are fortunate enough to witness an example like the one Jim set, be sure to discuss it with your son.

Walter Schirra Sr. said, "You don't raise heroes, you raise sons. And if you treat them like sons, they'll turn out to be heroes, even if it's just in your own eyes."[1] Boys have a way of becoming what you encourage them to be.

A man's primary role in life is to provide for and protect his family. That role requires that a man develop character in his life. Many of you reading this book have been involved with men who did not live up to their primary role in life. During seminars I always ask the single moms what qualities they think make a good man. They generally have some very good responses, often centering on the character traits missing from the men who've impacted their lives. Here's my list—in no particular order—compiled with help from the suggestions of many single moms. These are qualities that come to mind when I think of what a man is. Instill these qualities in your boy to help him become a good man.

## Perseverance

> It is not the critic who counts, not the man who points out how the strong man stumbled or where the doer of deeds could have done better.
>
> The credit belongs to the man who is actually in the arena; whose face is marred by dust and sweat and blood; who strives valiantly; who errs and comes short again and again; who knows the great enthusiasms, the great devotions, and spends himself in a worthy cause; who, at best, knows in the end the triumph of high achievement; and who, at the worst, if he fails, at least fails while daring

> greatly, so that his place shall never be with those cold and timid souls who know neither victory nor defeat.
>
> Theodore Roosevelt

The character trait of perseverance is fast becoming lost in our culture. I have owned my own business for fifteen years. During that time I have seen hundreds of businesses come and go in my own hometown. I truly believe I am still in business not because I am smarter or work harder or am luckier than anyone else (although I do believe that God's grace and blessings have played the biggest role in whatever success I have achieved) but because I have persevered during hard times.

Greatness is born by perseverance in the face of adversity. Few things worth doing are ever easy. As Calvin Coolidge said,

> Nothing in this world can take the place of persistence. Talent will not; nothing is more common than unsuccessful people with talent. Genius will not; unrewarded genius is almost a proverb. Education will not; the world is full of educated derelicts. Persistence and determination alone are omnipotent. The slogan "press on" has solved and always will solve the problems of the human race.[2]

Marriages and families also face hard times. Boys must learn to persevere in the face of adversity if they are to struggle forward later, during even tougher seasons of life. Perseverance is probably one of the toughest things for moms to teach their boys. It requires them to resist the urge to rescue their sons when they are struggling.

People today—men in particular—seem to quit more easily than they used to. They quit their jobs, they quit their marriages, they quit sports, they quit school, and they quit life whenever obstacles stand in their way or circumstances become too difficult. I've hired quite a number of young people straight out of college. They seem to believe they are entitled to the same pay, working conditions, and job status as their fathers, who have been in the workforce for twenty-five years. When that doesn't happen right away, they quit. In our era of instant gratification, the concept of paying one's dues has been lost in the rush to acquire as many material possessions as possible as quickly as possible.

In chapter 3 we discussed not letting boys become trained in the "art" of quitting. Perseverance is the art of *not* quitting. Help your son understand the rewards that await him by overcoming difficult circumstances.

Let your boy suffer if it means finishing a worthy task. I'm convinced we do our boys a grave disservice by saving them from every kind of suffering while they are growing up. While it's natural for a mom to want to try to keep her children from suffering, hardship tends to develop character all the same.

Perseverance is one of those qualities that builds strength of character. And really, when it's all said and done, the only thing a man has that can't be taken from him is his character.

## Loyalty

> The soul of me is very selfish. I have gone my way after a fashion that made me the center of the plan. And you who are so individual, who are so independent a spirit, whose

> soul is also a kingdom, have been so loyal, so forgiving, so self-sacrificing in your willingness to live my life. Nothing but love could have accomplished so wonderful a thing.
>
> Woodrow Wilson

The preceding quote was in a letter from Woodrow Wilson to his wife, Ellen Axson Wilson, dated September 23, 1913. Wilson's wife had wanted a career of her own, and Wilson was not ignorant of her self-sacrifice. This letter sums up his attitude toward his wife. A year later Ellen Wilson died.

It's interesting that Wilson equated forgiveness and self-sacrifice with loyalty. These are the characteristics many mothers exhibit toward their families.

I was stunned the first time I heard Stu Weber, the senior pastor at our church, say, "There are things worth dying for—things that are more important than life itself. Things like loyalty and freedom." He's right. There are things worth dying for—even today, especially today. It's just unpopular to say so in our current social climate.

How do you develop loyalty? You teach loyalty by being loyal. Does your son believe that you always have his best interests at heart—even when he's angry because you won't let him do what everybody else is doing? Does he know that you will stand by him even when everyone else is against him? Does he know that you would die for him? Make sure he knows. That's an important fact to know—that someone would be willing to die for us.

Wherever Ellen Wilson learned loyalty, she certainly showed it in such a fashion that Woodrow Wilson recognized it and cherished it in her.

God bless loyal people—I love loyal people. People who will stick with you when all else is in turmoil. People who will still love you even when they know you. People who, despite your human failures, still believe in you. Those are the kind of people I want in my life.

## Manners

> This is the final test of a gentleman: his respect for those who can be of no possible value to him.
>
> William Lyon Phelps

Teach your son how to treat others. Politeness is just plain good manners, and good manners never go out of style. Manners show respect for others, regardless of their status or attitude.

Perhaps the best model to hold up to boys is the Boy Scout credo: "On my honor I promise to be trustworthy, loyal, helpful, courteous, kind, obedient, cheerful, thrifty, brave, clean, and reverent." Not a bad model for a young man to aspire to, is it?

I believe each of us has been blessed by God with individual gifts. Some people have athletic ability, some have been blessed with intellect, others are great orators or writers, and some are destined to be great leaders. In trying to determine each of my children's God-given gifts, I've come to the belief that my son has been blessed with the gift of likability. Everywhere we go, whatever situation he is involved in, people like him and are drawn to him in a remarkably short period of time. I think, after observing this phenomenon for the past several years, that it is at least in part due to the fact that he is unfailingly polite and equally open to everyone—except his sister, of course.

Even when treated rudely, he continues to be polite to others, and they eventually respond in kind. I'm not sure how he learned to hone this gift (he certainly didn't catch it from me). Nevertheless, it works. Consequently, people want to spend time around him, are compelled to help him, and want to see him succeed. The gift of being polite and well mannered opens doors for him that might otherwise be closed and will probably help him to be successful throughout his lifetime, no matter what he chooses to accomplish.

### Courage

> The only thing necessary for the triumph of evil is for good men to do nothing.
>
> Edmund Burke

As stories began to emerge from the survivors of the South Tower of the World Trade Center, several people mentioned a mysterious young man who stepped out of the smoke and horror to lead them to safety. They did not know who this man was who saved their lives, but they did remember this: wrapped around his mouth and nose was a red bandanna.

For seventy-six minutes, the man in the red bandanna barked orders and led people down stairwells to safety. He said, "I found the stairs; follow me." He carried one woman down fifteen flights of stairs—on his back—while leading others to safety, urging them to keep going down. Then he headed back up the stairs.

Upstairs, a badly injured woman was sitting on a radiator when the man with the red bandanna over his face came running across the room and said, "Follow me. I know the way out. I will lead you to safety." Then he led several survivors to a stairwell that took them to safety. He was never seen alive again.

Six months later, on March 19, 2002, the body of the man with the red bandanna was found intact alongside the bodies of firefighters in a makeshift command center in the South Tower lobby buried under 110 stories of rubble.

Slowly the story began to come out. Welles Crowther graduated from Boston College, where he played lacrosse, always carrying his trademark red bandanna. His dad always carried a blue one. In high school Welles was the kid who would feed the puck to the hockey team's lowest-scoring player, hoping to give his teammate his first goal. At sixteen he became a junior volunteer firefighter, following in his dad's footsteps. After college he joined Sandler O'Neil and Partners and worked on the 104th floor of the South Tower. He always carried change to give to street people. His dream was to become a firefighter or public servant. On September 11, at the age of twenty-four, Welles Crowther became both, as well as a hero—the "man in the red bandanna."[3]

Welles Crowther showed one kind of courage—physical courage. Other kinds of courage are just as difficult and just as heroic. Courage is simply doing what needs to be done even though you're scared and tired.

Teach your son to lead courageously, to stand by his convictions even when they may result in pain, sorrow, or negative consequences. Someday he will lead his own family. Fathers are faced with tough decisions every day. The question is, do you want him to lead with courage or cowardice?

My daughter, Kelsey, is one of the bravest people I've ever met. She was born with a bilateral cleft lip. Her upper lip was open in two places, never having formed together, from the lip all the way up to her nose. She has undergone a total of six surgeries—the first at two months of age. If she was ever scared going into surgery, she never showed it. At age fifteen she has developed into a gorgeous young lady (funny how God works, isn't it?). However, she still has noticeable scars on her lip. Our family doesn't notice them, but rest assured, Kelsey does—especially through all the angst and self-consciousness of the teenage years.

A female friend of mine put Kelsey's dilemma into perspective for me. We were eating lunch one day, and she said, "I notice you have a cold sore on your lip. I bet you think everyone is looking at you, don't you?"

"I know they are," I replied.

"Well, then you've gotten just a small taste of what your daughter faces every day."

Wow! That comment really punched me in the gut. I finally came close to understanding my daughter's situation. Worst of all, I know she was subjected to cruel teasing from other kids during her primary school years.

What makes her so courageous? Despite knowing that everywhere she goes people will not only look at her lip but also ask about it, she still does not let it keep her from doing whatever she wants. She continues to expose herself to vulnerable situations, such as trying out for different sports, seeking out church activities, going to new schools, and attending summer camps—usually places where she doesn't know a soul. With the heart of a lion, she faces these fearful situations.

That's the kind of courage your son needs: the courage to continue to do what is right even when all those around him are calling for him to compromise. The courage to get up and go to work every day when he hates his job. The courage to stay married when it would be easier to run off with the woman from work who "really understands" him. The courage to live after a child has died. The courage to face, and possibly even overcome, a life-threatening disease. The courage to speak out against immorality when no one else seems to care. The courage to stand by his convictions in the face of overwhelming criticism.

## Compassion

> But when he was still a great way off, his father saw him and had compassion, and ran and fell on his neck and kissed him.
>
> Luke 15:20

Jesus tells the story of a man with two sons. One day the spoiled younger son said to his father, "Father, give me my inheritance now." So the father divided his estate and gave the younger son his portion.

Soon thereafter the younger son took all his possessions, cashed in his share of the estate, and ran off to the big city.

There he lived an extravagant lifestyle, wasting his wealth on immoral pursuits. Soon he had spent all of his money. A severe famine arose in the land, and he found himself starving. With no other choice, he became a servant to a local landowner. The landowner sent him into the fields to feed the swine, a heavy insult to his Jewish heritage. He was so hungry he would have eaten the slop he was feeding to the pigs, but no one would give him anything to eat. Finally he came to his senses and said, "How many of my father's hired servants have bread enough and to spare, and I perish with hunger! I will arise and go to my father, and will say to him, 'Father, I have sinned against heaven and before you, and I am no longer worthy to be called your son. Make me like one of your hired servants'" (Luke 15:17–19).

With that, he left and traveled to his father's home, a humiliated, filthy beggar. But while he was still far off, his father saw him and was filled with compassion. He ran and put his arms around him and kissed him. And the son said to him, "Father, I have sinned against heaven and in your sight, and am no longer worthy to be called your son" (v. 21).

But the father said to his servants, "Bring out the best robe and put it on him, and put a ring on his hand and sandals on his feet. And bring the fatted calf here and kill it, and let us eat and be merry" (vv. 22–23).

The older brother was in the field. As he neared the house, he heard music and dancing. He called one of the servants to him and asked what it meant. The servant said, "Your brother has come, and because he has received him safe and sound, your father has killed the fatted calf" (v. 27).

The older son grew angry and refused to attend his brother's party. His father came out and pleaded with him. He said to his father, "These many years I have been serving you; I never transgressed your commandment at any time; and yet you never gave me a young goat, that I might make merry with my friends. But as soon as this son of yours came, who has devoured your livelihood with harlots, you killed the fatted calf for him" (vv. 29–30).

The father replied, "Son, you are always with me, and all that I have is yours. It was right that we should make merry and be glad, for your brother was dead and is alive again, and was lost and is found" (vv. 31–32).

This story illustrates the aspect of forgiveness found in compassion. Another aspect of compassion for men is safeguarding the weak.

Is there anything worse than a bully? Is there anything less manly than a thug who picks on those weaker than himself? Point out everyday examples of bullies, and explain to your son the ramifications for everyone involved in each scenario. Use examples such as the mugger who steals old people's social security checks, the husband who physically or emotionally abuses his wife and children, or the boss who verbally or sexually harasses an employee.

A man should defend those who cannot defend themselves. Teach your boy early in life the nobility of protecting the weak and helpless.

It's pretty normal for boys to get into playground scuffles from time to time. Most mothers become quite upset when their sons are involved in these skirmishes. However, without advocating violence, I believe there are times when a male—man or boy—must defend himself or those who are helpless.

Let's imagine for a moment that your seven-year-old son is at school one day. The classroom bully has decided to pick on the smallest boy in the class—one who also has several physical challenges, which prevent him from running away or defending himself. Everyone in the school is afraid of this bully, because he's larger, stronger, and more aggressive than any of the other kids. School authorities have suspended him several times.

On this particular day your son notices a crowd of kids just off school grounds. As he approaches he notices that the bully and his cronies have the small boy in the middle of a circle and are taking turns pushing him and verbally abusing him. The level of violence is escalating to the point where the pushes are becoming punches of greater and greater intensity as the small boy can only cry in his fear and frustration. Your son realizes there are no adults around to help.

Your son knows that if someone does not do something, the small boy could be severely injured. Swallowing his fear, your son steps forward and says, "Knock it off! Leave him alone!" Now the bully and his flunkies turn toward your son like a pack of hyenas. The bully soon attacks, and your son has no choice but to defend himself as best he can. A teacher finally arrives and hauls both boys off to the principal's office, where they are suspended for fighting.

How would you handle this situation?

A wise mother lets her son know that while she doesn't condone fighting, under those circumstances, she's proud of his actions. Also, he should be allowed to suffer the consequences of his actions (suspension from school for fighting) without your intervention. No, it's probably not fair under the circumstances, but life's not fair, and the suspension reinforces that there are consequences to his actions. This will cause him to think through such situations in the future and not just react emotionally. This is also a good opportunity to talk to him about other ways to respond when he finds himself in a similar situation in the future.

## Self-Discipline and Self-Control

> I think of discipline as the continual everyday process of helping a child learn self-discipline.
>
> Fred Rogers

Self-discipline and self-control are different yet inexplicably interwoven. Self-discipline is doing something we don't want to do but should. Self-control is not doing something we want to do but shouldn't. The lack of one or both of these character traits sinks more men and destroys more lives than any other character deficit. The absence of either of these traits leads men into addictions to drugs, gambling, pornography, drinking, and adultery—all of which are family destroyers and soul killers.

Self-discipline and self-control keep a man from doing things in private that he would never do in public. They are inner strengths a man develops over time with exercise, like a muscle. Typically, if a man lacks self-discipline in one area of his life, he lacks self-control in other areas of his life as well.

How does a boy develop self-discipline and self-control? He develops them by being held accountable for his actions. If his going to a movie is predicated upon his cleaning his room and he doesn't clean it, then he can't go to the movie. If you tell him he can't have any ice cream if he doesn't eat his dinner, then no ice cream if he doesn't eat his dinner—even if the rest of his siblings get ice cream. If he's disrespectful to you, he doesn't get to watch television that night. Stick to your guns, even if it's been a while since the infraction and he's been well behaved during the interim. If you give in, you've lost. Once he knows he's not accountable for his actions, you've lost his respect and any control you had over him. He might throw a fit or make things uncomfortable for a while, but once he learns that you mean what you say, he'll accept it. Hang in there. If circumstances dictate, all of us are capable of enduring more than we think possible. It might not be easy or comfortable, but it's possible.

I once saw an episode of the television program *Cops* where a seven-year-old boy being raised by his mother locked her out of the house. The police had to break down the door and forcibly make the boy obey his mother. It was terribly embarrassing to watch this small boy terrorize his mother and stymie two full-grown policemen. It was a perfect example of a boy without any accountability in his life.

Think of the men in your life who have let you down, and see if the words *self-discipline* or *self-control* come to mind when you say their names. In this instant-gratification world we live in, self-control and self-discipline may be the greatest gifts you can give your son as he grows into manhood.

## Dependability

Can he be counted on? Is his word his bond? Are his wife, children, and friends confident that he will be there for them when times are tough? A man who is dependable can be counted on to do what is best for you and others around him.

Your son needs to understand that no man is an island. His choices and the decisions he makes affect other people's lives whether he is willing to admit it or not. Our decisions impact others' lives like a pebble dropping in a pond creates ripples across the surface. When your boy becomes a father, his decisions will create ripples in peoples' lives for generations thereafter.

## Honesty

> But you must pay for conformity. All goes well as long as you run with conformists. But you, who are honest men in other particulars, know, that there is alive somewhere a man whose honesty reaches to this point also, that he shall not kneel to false gods, and, on the day when you meet him, you sink into the class of counterfeits.
>
> Ralph Waldo Emerson

The dictionary defines *honest* as "free from deception, truthful, genuine, real, reputable, credible, marked by integrity, frank, upright, just, conscientious, honorable."

One of the hardest things for men to do is admit when they are wrong. While that's probably not earth-shattering news to most of you, be aware that boys struggle with the same natural inclination. Men are taught from a young age to always be right, to know how to fix things, to have all the answers. It's a heavy burden—one that is compounded when men are not honest enough with themselves and others to admit they are human. Men fall into a trap of believing they have to be perfect. It's a no-win situation, and we can start remedying the problem by teaching boys how to admit when they are wrong. Males have a much easier time being truthful with others if they are honest with themselves first.

In order to do this, a boy needs to learn about his own individual strengths and weaknesses. Some weaknesses, such as a lustful nature, are inherent in most men. By being honest with himself, a boy can be aware of potential character pitfalls. For example, most people would consider me to be a diligent, hardworking man. And I am—but only because I know myself to be lazy by nature. I force myself to work hard (through self-discipline), because I know that if I don't, my natural inclination toward laziness will surface and prevent me from fulfilling the destiny God has planned for me.

Talk to your son about his God-given strengths and weaknesses. When my son, Frank, was in the later elementary school years, it became apparent that he probably would not become a star athlete. Not because he wasn't physically capable or coordinated enough but because he did not seem to have the drive or competitive desire—the "fire in the belly," if you will. Rather than force him to be a sports star (as was my initial inclination), I chose to focus on his strengths. Frank was very intelligent and loved music. I encouraged him to join the band and learn a musical instrument. I said, "You know, when I was in high school, I'd look up into the stands, and those guys in the band always seemed to be having such a good time. Plus, they get to hang out around the cheerleaders and get out of school and travel to all the games." Whenever we watched college basketball or football games on television, I was quick to point out the camera shots of the band members goofing around with their faces painted. I also casually mentioned that the band members get into all the games free and that if they play for a college that is a national powerhouse, they get to attend championship games most people never will.

Frank joined the band in sixth grade and has continued playing in the band up into college. He has enjoyed himself immensely and has learned to play several instruments that will give him joy throughout his life. His experiences were positive in nature, which allowed him to develop a healthy self-esteem, whereas he might have struggled with his self-image had he been pushed into sports.

Let your son know early on that you expect honesty from him at all times—then model that behavior yourself. A man who is honest with himself is honest to others. Little white lies to protect someone's feelings are not necessarily innocent. The art of diplomacy and good manners will serve your son better than a small lie.

### Humility

Life is a long lesson in humility.

James M. Barrie

Most young men are filled with pride—I was. Humility allows men to achieve great things for a purpose higher than themselves. This includes putting their family's well-being ahead of their own wants and desires.

Humility seems to have a bad rap today. If someone, especially a man, is called humble or exhibits humility, the connotation is that he is a wimp. Humility is somehow associated with being humiliated, while pride is looked upon as a virtue. Young men are supposed to be confident, cocky, overachieving go-getters—to never admit they're wrong. However, *The Merriam-Webster Dictionary* defines *humble* as (1) "not proud or haughty," (2) "not pretentious; unassuming," (3) "modest."

All in all, those are pretty good character traits. Some of the wisest, happiest, and most successful men I know are extremely humble individuals.

Humility is the opposite of pride. The Bible says about pride, "Pride goes before destruction, and a haughty spirit before a fall" (Prov. 16:18); and about pride versus humility, "A man's pride will bring him low, but the humble in spirit will retain honor" (Prov. 29:23).

The older I get, the more stock I put in humility. Maybe it's because humility comes with maturity.

## Trustworthiness

> You shall select from all the people able men, such as fear God, men of truth, hating covetousness; and place such over them to be rulers of thousands, rulers of hundreds, rulers of fifties, and rulers of tens. And let them judge the people at all times. Then it will be that every great matter they shall bring to you, but every small matter they themselves shall judge.
>
> Exodus 18:21–22

To trust someone is to know that he will stand beside you—that he won't cut and run when the going gets tough. Author Preston Gillham says, "Trust is the confidence that continues to believe, even if what you believe appears to be untrue. To my way of thinking, trust is one step deeper than faith."[4]

One of the ways I determine a man's character is whether I would trust him to cover my back in battle. Some people (usually men I wouldn't trust in battle) have commented that it's a harsh way to judge someone, but I don't think it is. We are in a war—a spiritual war—and we need people around us we can trust to cover our backs, people who put our well-being ahead of their own.

Talk to your son about what being able to trust someone means to you. If you have trouble trusting due to past experiences, discuss it with him so he can understand how strong a character trait trustworthiness is and how damaging it can be when violated.

## Honor

> Reputation is what other people know about you. Honor is what you know about yourself.
>
> Lois McMaster Bujold, *A Civil Campaign*

In the movie *Rob Roy*, Liam Neeson plays Robert Roy McGregor, a clan chieftain in the early 1800s Scottish Highlands. At the beginning of the movie, Rob Roy has the following conversation with his two young sons about honor:

Son: "Father, will McGregors ever be kings again?"
RR: "All men with honor are kings. But not all kings have honor."
Son: "What is honor?"
RR: "Honor is . . . what no man can give you and none can take away. Honor is a man's gift to himself."
Son: "Do women have it?"
RR: "Women are the heart of honor, and we cherish and protect it in them. You must never mistreat a woman or malign a man, or stand by and see another do so."
Son: "How do you know if you have it?"
RR: "Never worry on the getting of it. It grows in you and speaks to you. All you need do is listen."

I want my son to have honor. To stand tall as the fierce winds of adversity blow around him. To cherish and protect women and children. To fight for justice and equality. To stand for *something*.

In this chapter we discussed some of the qualities boys need to develop in order to reach their potential as men. This is not an exhaustive list, nor can you reasonably expect your son to master all of the traits summarized here. However, by being aware of which character traits you admire in men, you can help your son see them in others and develop them as he grows older.

## Questions for Discussion

1. Make a list of character traits you want your son to have. Discuss with other mothers why these traits

are important in general and to you in particular. How can you help install these traits in your son?

2. Think of the best example you've witnessed of manly behavior and discuss it with your son.
3. Tell your son what you think makes a man. Ask him what character traits he thinks are manly.

# 8

# Respect

> The principal thing children are taught by hearing these lullabies is respect. They are taught to respect certain things in life and certain people. By giving respect, they hope to gain self-respect and through self-respect, they gain the respect of others. Self-respect is one of the qualities my people stress and try to nurture, and one of the controls an Indian has as he grows up. Once you lose your self-respect, you just go down.
>
> *Henry Old Coyote,* Respect for Life

There's an old saying that goes, "In order to get respect you have to earn it." But in order to get respect or even earn respect, you must have respect for yourself first. Unfortunately, self-respect is acquired by receiving respect from others whose opinion you value. It's sort of a catch-22 situation, like a dog chasing his tail in a circle, round and round until he collapses from exhaustion.

I believe you get respect by treating others with respect. Yes, there are many times when people behave in a manner not deserving of respect, but I think respect is a fundamental need of human beings. Once their need for it is met, it's easier for them to offer it back.

Being respectful toward people does not mean being scared of or subservient toward them. It merely means treating them as you would like to be treated and extending to them the dignity any human being deserves as one of God's creations.

## Respect for Women

> Every gentleman is a man, but not every man is a gentleman.
>
> Author unknown

Boys need to be taught to respect women of all ages—girls to grandmothers. They should open doors and carry heavy items for them, not because women are weaker or incapable, but because they deserve to be honored and cherished. This may be politically incorrect, but it's true.

Teach your boy at a young age to open the door for you and for his sisters. As courtesy and respect manifest themselves in other areas of his life, they will become a lifelong habit and will help create an attitude that some future young lady will greatly appreciate and praise you for.

A number of years ago, I began opening my wife's car door for her every time we got in the car. Throughout our marriage, I'd usually opened doors for her but not often her car door. I did this to start honoring her in public and for my kids' benefit—so they could see how a man should treat a woman. I must admit, it felt a bit "courtly" or old-fashioned at first. Now I do it naturally and still receive quite a few curious glances from people. But I've noticed that younger women especially seem to like it. Hopefully, this example will spur young men toward similar respectful behavior. If nothing else, it has caused my daughter to expect young men to open doors for her and influenced my son to be chivalrous with females as well.

Boys also need to be taught how to love a woman. If you're divorced, perhaps your former marriage was not a good example of a man and woman's relationship. Your relationship with your son is the first context in which he can learn to value a woman. We tend to treasure things that have great value and treat them with gentleness and respect. Teach your sons the value of women. Whether you believe it or not, as a mother, you are more valuable than you will ever know. Talk to him about what things are important to women and what things cause them pain.

## Single Moms and Self-Respect

After the emotional wreckage caused by a divorce, some women find themselves struggling with low self-esteem. Single mothers often find themselves in an overwhelming situation that causes them to function in a survival mode. Unfortunately, the constant pressures of living in a continuous survival mode lead some women to eventually shut down—either focusing entirely on their own needs (either through male companionship or other forms of relief, such as partying) or losing their will to continue altogether. The single mothers who do continue the struggle, who read books and discover they've been codependent or have been operating in some other form of dysfunctionality, enter into a self-sufficiency mode. They dig themselves into this pit deeper and deeper, gravitating toward other single mothers to share support, shopping, cooking, and child care. These women often don't realize that they have lost balance in their family lives and that they haven't made time for healthy relationships for their kids to emulate. One former single mother told me, "It's a humbling moment when you realize that you can't raise a child alone."

In addition, many women, even those with healthy self-esteem, tend to put themselves last and defer to everyone else in their relationships. A female friend of mine believes this is because women sometimes *like* to play the role of martyr.

So if a woman has been in an abusive relationship, how can she promote respect for women, especially when she has modeled acceptance of lack of respect or has been forced into a situation where she had to sacrifice her self-respect? As it was put to me by one mother, "If I have been the lowest rung on the family ladder and have been the doormat in my previous relationship, how do I teach my son to treat me and other women with respect?"

First of all, it's important for your son's sake, as well as your own, that you get help in dealing with issues of low

**Rhonda's Story**

Rhonda's mother found herself pregnant at sixteen, dropped out of high school, and got married. After three years her alcoholic husband left her. Rhonda's mother suddenly found herself a single mother without a high school diploma raising two little girls. Rhonda's first stepfather was a man raised in an alcoholic home. Years later, as an adult, Rhonda found herself married to a man of an alcoholic upbringing as well. "I was afraid of men," she said. Two years later they had a baby girl, and several years after that, in an attempt to save their marriage, they adopted a baby boy.

"I wanted a picture-perfect family," Rhonda said. "But with each of us being raised in dysfunctional families, we just didn't have the coping skills to make good choices." After twelve years of marriage, Rhonda's husband left her and the kids with a mountain of debt. "I lived in constant fear—what if I get sick?" She was also angry. "That was the last thing I wanted for my kids," she says.

After four years of single motherhood, a white knight came charging to her rescue in the form of a financially secure man. "He was a savior. He treated me and my son like royalty." However, after several years the honeymoon wore thin. "The pressures of a blended family along with his unresolved tensions from a previous marriage were just too much," Rhonda says. Soon he began drinking heavily and becoming abusive to both Rhonda and her son. After seven years of marriage, Rhonda again found herself a single mother. She says, "My self-esteem was so low. I felt such a sense of failure." Even though she was miserable being married to a potentially dangerous man, she still wasn't happy about the divorce. "This definitely wasn't in my plan."

Rhonda's advice to other women who find themselves in her situation: "I had to spend a lot of time reading and talking to a counselor in order to overcome my low self-esteem. Now I spend a part of each day connecting with God through prayer and meditation." Rhonda believes that the best thing she has done for her kids is to heal herself. "My kids see that I learned from my mistakes. By helping others, I have improved my own wisdom and strength of character. I try to put myself in my children's shoes and make decisions based on choices I would've wanted my mother to make." Lastly, she says, "The most important message I would like to give others is forgiveness. Forgive yourselves for mistakes and forgive your ex. It is in the forgiveness that light can come back into your life."

self-worth. You must like yourself before others can realize your value. Find a Christian counselor to help you work through the issues you may be having in these areas. I suggest a Christian counselor not just because of my own personal religious beliefs but because all wisdom is based on biblical principles. My wife and I have attended many counseling sessions over the years, both before and after I became a Christian. The counselors who have helped me (and our marriage) the most have all been Christians.

One of the struggles single mothers often face is feelings of resentment. Prior to submitting this book for publication, I asked several moms of boys to review it for me. My friend Daina is a former single mom who told me while reviewing this manuscript, "Keep in mind that even the best of us hold some form of resentment for the absent male, and that transfers into defensiveness. As hard as I have tried to forgive and let go of the resentments toward my ex-husband's lack of parenting, I still battle with it, and it transforms into resentment even toward Scott [current husband] or even my children sometimes. I know that I am not being totally fair, but it is at an emotional level." Very well said. Realizing these feelings and how they contribute to your overall mental health is the first step in the healing process.

I understand that you may not feel like you have the time to fit one more commitment such as a counseling appointment into your schedule. But realizing your self-worth and value is fundamental to creating a healthy family life for your children. It should take priority over other commitments, at least in the short term. Heal yourself so you can heal others.

Stephanie Martson, a family therapist, says in her book *The Magic of Encouragement,* "When children are treated with respect, they conclude that they deserve respect and hence develop self-respect. When children are treated with acceptance, they develop self-acceptance; when they are cherished, they conclude that they deserve to be loved, and they develop self-esteem."[1]

Your son can fall into the same feelings of low self-esteem and low self-worth due to the loss of his father and family structure. Without your healing guidance, he will struggle to overcome these hurdles. Once he reaches manhood, these feelings of inferiority become much more difficult to overcome and manifest themselves in a variety of dysfunctional behaviors.

Change is difficult, and it takes a lot of hard work. Unfortunately, change doesn't happen overnight; it often takes a long time to see significant differences in our lives. That's why most people choose not to grow, even if they're unhappy. You need to leave your comfort zone if necessary to develop a healthy self-respect for a higher purpose—to develop a man who will treat women with respect and dignity.

## Boundaries

> Children can't make their own rules and no child is happy without them. The great need of the young is for authority that protects them against the consequences of their own primitive passions and their lack of experience, that provides them with guides for everyday behavior and that builds some solid ground they can stand on for the future.
>
> Leontine Young, *Life among the Giants*

Kids today, especially those from single-parent homes, need boundaries more than ever before. Why? Because they tend to be on their own more often. This gives them the opportunity, or even forces them, to make decisions they have no prior experience or guidance with.

Set acceptable boundaries on your son's behavior. The number one boundary is that being disrespectful to Mom is not acceptable! How you allow your son to treat you is how he will treat his wife. You're also training your daughters (and other young girls within your sphere of influence) how to expect to be treated in their relationships.

Much like teaching discipline, creating boundaries for your son is a way of civilizing him. As Dr. James Dobson says in *Bringing Up Boys*, "A stream without banks becomes a swamp. It is your job as parents to build the channel in which the stream will run."[2]

As my son entered adolescence, hormones he hadn't yet learned to control kicked in. One day he naturally got a little mouthy with his mother. Luckily, I happened to overhear his disrespect. I immediately got in his face and said, "That's my wife you're talking to. I wouldn't let another man talk to her that way, and I'm sure not going to allow you to talk to her that way." That one time seems to have done the trick. Not that he hasn't gotten lippy now and then—but when he starts to and sees me look at him, he seems to remember our conversation and makes the effort to control his mouth. (This is an example of his using self-discipline to avoid unpleasant consequences.) You might try showing your son the unpleasant consequences he can expect if he becomes disrespectful toward you.

I make it a practice to say something whenever I see a boy being disrespectful to his mother in public. If his father's not around and his mother doesn't correct him, I will look him in the eyes and quietly but gruffly say, "Hey! Don't be disrespectful to your mother!" Usually, the boy is surprised and has a rather shameful look on his face. Believe it or not, I have had mothers who got angry and told me to mind my own business! Mostly, though, moms seem grateful for the help. If your son is being disrespectful to you and you don't put him in his place, don't get upset if a man does. Boys need to be held accountable by men, especially in the area of respecting women. All too often men don't fulfill this responsibility, which is why there are so many tragic examples of boys and men going astray and abusing women and children in our society today. As men, we seem to have lost the ability, or maybe the desire, to police our own gender.

## Questions for Discussion

1. Have your previous relationships caused you to question your worth as a human being?
2. In what ways can you proactively teach your son to respect women and all living beings?
3. What types of boundaries have you established to control your son's behavior? What behaviors does he exhibit that still need boundaries?

# 9

# The Importance of Male Role Models

> You have just finished a run, and you are sitting on the porch sweating like a horse and smelling like one, and your son, or perhaps a little neighbor boy, sits down next to you, leans against you, and says, "You smell good." This is the primal longing for one's father.
>
> *Kent Hughes,* Disciplines of a Godly Man

Boys learn to become men from other men. Masculinity bestows masculinity. Femininity can never bestow masculinity. John Eldredge says, "A boy learns who he is and what he's got from a man, or the company of men. He cannot learn it from any other place. He cannot learn it from other boys, and he cannot learn it from the world of women."[1] Bestowing masculinity requires active intervention in a boy's life by an adult male. Without that intervention in the form of a role model, boys are like ships without rudders, tossed about whichever way the wind and waves throw them.

In her book *Between Mothers and Sons: The Making of Vital and Loving Men*, Evelyn Bassoff, Ph.D., contends that when boys have no flesh-and-blood men with whom to identify, they may turn for inspiration to the pitiful he-man images the popular media promotes. Or they turn to neighborhood gang leaders or criminals whose brutality they mistake for true masculinity.[2]

Boys have a void in their souls that asks, "Am I a man? How will I know?" Writing about the deepest question in a boy's heart, Eldredge says, "It's not a question—it's *the* question, the one every boy and man is longing to ask. Do I have what it takes? Am I powerful? Until a man *knows* he's a man, he will forever be trying to prove he is one, while at the same time shrink from anything that might reveal he is not. Most men live their lives haunted by that question, or crippled by the answer they've been given."[3]

Boys need that void filled by the actions and blessings of a man. A woman can tell her son all day long that he is normal, that his body parts are the right size and shape, and he will never truly believe her. But when an adult male answers the questions deep in the boy's heart, the answers will be readily, and with relief, believed. Robert Bly, in *Iron John*, says, "Only men can initiate men, as only women can initiate women. Women can change the embryo to a boy, but only men can change the boy to a man."[4]

Boys who don't receive this blessing from their fathers are wounded deeply. Of course, most men I know deny that they have been wounded—just as men are taught to do—but the wounds are there just the same. Boys, however, who spend time with their fathers or other adult males, working, playing, going to ball games, or just fishing, receive the blessing of masculinity.

I was raised by a stepfather, but I met my biological father at the age of twenty-four. We have since developed a strong father-son relationship. This past year I received a Father's Day card from him. Like most men, I don't normally care much for greeting cards. But this card grabbed me by the lapels and shook me. The card read:

> Son, you're a blessing. You've always been a blessing to the family. . . . You took the Lord into your heart and have grown in His love. Now you do so much to praise Him in the way you live and in the things you do. It has been a joy to watch you grow, and this comes with so much pride in the special man you have become.

After that this reserved, taciturn man wrote, "Rick, always remember I love you and am proud of you. Dad." Even now that I am forty-seven, my dad's blessing means so much to me.

When we do not provide our adolescent boys with elders to become friends with, when we do not help guide them in their choice of friends, when we allow overreliance on the media to distract them from the bonding process, and when we push them (or allow them to gravitate) toward female bonding before they are emotionally ready (e.g., letting them date before they are sixteen or so), we make their emotional disadvantage into nearly an assurance of lifelong emotional immaturity.[5]

## The Need to See What to Be

> Boys become men by watching men, by standing close to men. Manhood is a ritual passed from generation to generation with precious few spoken instructions. Passing the torch of manhood is a fragile, tedious task. If the rite of passage is successfully completed, the boy-become-man is like an oak of hardwood character. His shade and influence will bless all those who are fortunate enough to lean on him and rest under his canopy.
>
> Preston Gillham, *Lifetime Guarantee*

The above quote by Preston Gillham emphasizes what it takes to create a productive man and identifies the impact men have on boys.

Because males are visual creatures, they need to see models and examples of what a man looks like, how he acts in certain situations, and how he carries himself.

In *Man Enough*, Frank Pittman states:

> Masculinity is supposed to be passed on from father to son. Women, no matter how wonderful, no matter how loving, can't teach it to us. If we don't have fathers, we should have grandfathers, uncles, stepfathers to raise us from boys into men. If we don't have men in our family, then our need for mentors begins early. If the males we know are the other teenage boys or the macho heroes from the movies, we may get a distorted, exaggerated concept of masculinity.[6]

Fathering, like mothering, is a daunting and complex task. It's complicated by the world we live in, with its increasing expectations, tight economics, and competing pressures. Fathering is also complicated by men's relationships with their own fathers, many of whom were physically absent or emotionally distant.[7]

Further complications arise because fathering is a learned trait, one that men aren't typically born with. Without a positive role model early in life, it's extremely difficult for a boy to learn how to be a man, father, or husband, or even how to love his wife.

One of the toughest tasks I faced as a young father was where to find information on fathering or being a husband, or even being a man. Some of you are probably saying that women are not born knowing how to be mothers either. Maybe so, but it's been my experience that women seem to be more intuitively equipped to nurture and raise children. I was raised in an alcoholic home by my mother and stepfather. My wife's father abandoned the family sometime around her birth, and she was raised (to the age of thirteen) by an uninvolved mother. Consequently, neither my wife nor I had particularly positive parenting role models—my wife's worse than mine—yet my wife seemed more naturally proficient than I was in parenting our children when they were born.

It was 1986, and I anxiously awaited the birth of our first child. My wife and I waited for five years after our wedding to have a child, ostensibly because I wanted to own a home. In reality, I think I knew in my heart that I wasn't mature enough to handle the responsibilities of fatherhood. Our son, Frank, was twenty days past due and, having large shoulders, became stuck in the birth canal. To my shock, the midwife just grabbed him by the head, braced her feet, and popped him out like a champagne cork. I was flushed with joy as my son welcomed life with a screaming breath. But on the way home, thoughts flashed through my mind. *Wait a second. I've never been trained for this. I've trained for my career, and I've trained for sports. I even attended all of the Lamaze classes, but no one has ever taught me how to be a father.* A sobering weight of responsibility descended upon my shoulders. I knew I was responsible for an innocent, defenseless life I had helped create. But I didn't know what to do.

I think most men feel this panic when faced with the responsibility of raising a child. Some cut and run from that panic, and some accept the responsibility. I suspect that most of the men who run in panic are the ones who had that behavior modeled for them by other males early in life.

## Mentors

> It is my God-appointed task to ensure that my sons will be ready to lead a family. I must equip them to that end. Little boys are the hope of the next generation. They are the fathers of tomorrow. They must know who they are and what they are to do. They must see their role model in action.
>
> Steve Farrar, *Point Man*

Boys need role models. In the absence of a father in the home, or in the case of an uninvolved father, the task of

**Shirley's Story**

Four years ago Shirley was in her midthirties with two sons, ages eleven and thirteen, when her husband decided he had to follow his obsession with living life as a woman. After leaving the family, Shirley's ex-husband maintained contact with the boys for about one year . . . until they discovered his secret. As Shirley explained, "Because they were at a pivotal time in their sexual development, I think the boys were scared that their father's gender confusion would rub off on them. I just tried to assure them that their father's sexual identity was no reflection upon them or who they were."

Shirley says that the hardest part of the whole ordeal was letting the boys think through and process the situation for themselves. "Being a mother, I had a natural tendency to rush in and save them from suffering. I felt like pressuring them to talk about it, but that's the way women process feelings, not boys. I had to back off and not try and fix things for them."

Shirley says the presence of her church's youth pastor was a blessing. "This wonderful man played a pivotal role in the boys' lives. He was an excellent male role model and gave them a man to talk to. Also, it helped that each boy had close friends that came from intact families with good dads."

Shirley says she tried to raise the boys as honestly as possible while modeling humility. "There were times when I just had to say, 'I'm sorry—I goofed again. This is a very hard time for me. Please forgive me.'"

Shirley's advice to mothers who find themselves in a similar situation is this: "The most important thing is not to give up. You think you are never going to live through it, but you will. Make sure the boys have male role models in their lives. Also, use a teamwork approach. I gave them the expectation of helping out around the house, because I just couldn't do everything myself. While that was difficult, I think the experience taught the boys to be self-sufficient."

The boys are sixteen and eighteen years of age now. The oldest begins seminary in the fall.

finding those role models falls to Mom. You have to find ways to make sure your sons see a role model in action.

Children without fathers need men to step forward as positive influences in their lives. The plight of many single mothers is the challenge of finding men willing to fill those roles for their sons and daughters. Young men without exposure to mature male leadership can become predators. Young women who have been abandoned by their fathers often try to find the paternal love and attention they desperately require in the wrong places—like the backseat of a car.

Older men have a responsibility to walk alongside younger men, giving them the benefit of their experience. Likewise, young men should be open—in fact, eager—to receive advice from the more mature members of their sex. Too often, however, male pride stops them from sharing and receiving this crucial information.

Ideally, your son's father is actively involved in his life. If not, you must find positive male role models to fill that void. It's not easy, but with some work, you can find men who will help mentor your son. Boy Scouts of America leaders, Little League and soccer coaches, and male teachers may all provide good male role modeling and mentoring. However, it's important that you make these men aware that your son's father is not involved in his life so they will understand their importance in your son's life. Grandfathers, uncles, neighbors, and your son's friends' fathers are also candidates. Again, explain to them specifically why you would like them involved in your son's life. As we discussed earlier in this book, men don't always pick up on the obvious, especially in relationships.

Ask your male neighbor, "The next time you take your son to the ball game, will you ask my son to come?" or "The next time you mow the lawn, can my son help?" Also, contact the pastor at your local church. Churches are filled with men who would love to help a fatherless lad. Helping widows and orphans is a biblical mandate. Though he may not technically qualify, your son is an orphan for all practical purposes as far as his father's absence is concerned.

Men are probably not going to walk up to you and ask if they can be involved in your son's life. In fact, I'd be nervous if one did. In these times, a man may even be reluctant to spend any time at all around a child who is not his own. The reality is, guilty or innocent, even the accusation of impropriety will ruin a man's career, family, and reputation—in short, his whole life. Therefore, it's vitally important that you be the catalyst that brings the adult male into your son's life.

Likewise, it's also your obligation to ensure your son's protection. How do you bring adult males into his life and make sure he's safe? Perhaps, at least initially, it would be beneficial to get your family and the man's family involved together in a variety of activities. That may require discussing the situation ahead of time with the man and his wife so that everyone clearly understands your agenda. Also, I'd make sure that the man has children close to your son's age so they can attend events together as a group.

Find activities to attend in which men are involved. One single mom I know brings her young boy to our men's basketball games each week. We've unofficially adopted him as our team mascot. He sits on the bench during the game and runs around during warm-ups. This way he's exposed to a variety of different types of men and is able to see how they react in a wide range of situations. He also gets to see us at our best and worst—in a stressful, competitive environment.

Look for good boys to be your son's friends. I think it's important for parents to take an active interest in directing their children into friendships that will be healthy and nurturing. It's equally important that the families of your son's friends have the same vision and values as you do. That requires you to meet and know the parents of your son's friends.

Also, find other women associated with good boys, and offer support to each other. Being a mother is incredibly wearying, even more so for a single mother. It's a tough job, and you need encouragement. Try to stay close to your family or good friends. If you walk this path alone, there will be no one to pick you up when you fall—and we all fall sometimes. See if you can find a group of mothers to meet periodically for support and encouragement.

## Heroes

### Great Men

Not gold, but only man can make
A people great and strong;
Men who, for truth and honor's sake,
Stand fast and suffer long.
Brave men who work while others sleep,
Who dare while others fly—
They build a nation's pillars deep
And lift them to the sky.

Ralph Waldo Emerson

Hold up male heroes for your son; he needs to see what they look like. Heroes need not be famous, larger-than-life action figures. They can be the average guy down the street who gets up every day and goes to work at a job he dislikes just to support his family. Occasionally, the newspaper or a magazine will have an article about a man who has lived a heroic life or has committed an act of heroism. Books and movies provide a source of heroes you can use to supplement other sources. Unfortunately, movies today that provide positive male role models are few and far between. Look for movies with men who have good moral convictions and stand for strong values. I still get goose bumps watching Mel Gibson as William Wallace in *Braveheart*. It inspires me every time I hear him say, "And dying in your beds, many years from now, would you be willing to trade all the days from this day to that to come back here and tell our enemies that they may take our lives, but they'll never take our freedom!"

One of the best movies I've seen that illustrates the need a boy has for an older male in his life is *Secondhand Lions*. In one heart-wrenching scene, Haley Joel Osment begs Robert Duvall to stay alive long enough to give him his "what every boy needs to hear to become a man" speech.

Here are some more inspirational "guy" movies. Many of these movies you might not enjoy, but I suspect your son will be very excited about them. Make sure they're age appropriate for your son: *The Jackie Robinson Story*; *Master and Commander*, starring Russell Crowe; *The Last Samurai*, starring Tom Cruise; *The Last of the Mohicans*, starring Daniel Day Lewis; *The Patriot*, starring Mel Gibson; *Remember the Titans*, starring Denzel Washington; *Hoosiers*, starring Gene Hackman; *Rudy*, starring Sean Astin; *Lonesome Dove*, starring Robert Duvall; *Glory*, starring Matthew Broderick; *Gladiator*, starring Russell Crowe; *Signs*, starring Mel Gibson; *We Were Soldiers*, starring Mel Gibson; and of course, the granddaddy of all guy movies, *Braveheart*, starring Mel Gibson. Any of the Lord of the Rings, Star Wars, or Indiana Jones movies are also fun for boys. At the end of this book, I've included a list of movies you can use to expose your son to strong male role models.

Give books as presents to your son. Not just one book, but five or six at a time. The trick is to find books written at a level that is not too difficult yet is sufficiently challenging to be of interest. Remember, they need to be adventurous, with swashbuckling sword fighting and a good dose of action. Give books in conjunction with other gifts. If you give him a basketball, include a book about a famous basketball player. If you give him a baseball glove, give him a book about a baseball star. Whatever his interests may be—dinosaurs, geology, insects, snakes, rodeos, trains, race cars, music, or art—find a book about someone he can look up to in that arena. "Eyewitness" types of books provide a wealth of information on almost any subject along with interesting pictures and facts.

Books about our founding fathers, pioneers, frontiersmen (Davy Crockett, Daniel Boone, Jim Bowie, Kit Carson), cowboys (Wild Bill Hickock, Buffalo Bill, Wyatt Earp), soldiers (all the way from ancient times to the present), and athletes generally present good role models with the action boys like. Boys crave heroes.

Boys are typically not readers. However, our culture does not do much to encourage them to be readers. Encourage your son to read; it is a wonderful gift he will appreciate for a lifetime.

Some ways to encourage your son are to let him see you reading and to leave books lying around the house. Often, boys are teased about reading. In those cases, reading may be a private activity for him. Respect that he may not want to talk about everything he reads or even be praised for reading. Encourage relatives and family friends your son loves and admires (especially older males) to give books as presents. Let your child make choices at the library or bookstore, and don't criticize his interests.

Recognize that reading about information is as legitimate as reading novels. Acknowledge this fact to your son when he follows written instructions for a hobby or reads the sports pages. Some boys love acquiring facts or trivia and especially enjoy the *Guinness Book of World Records*, the *World Almanac*, or sports almanacs just for the fun of browsing through them. Get your son his own library card at an early age.

Also, audio books appeal to males. The local library usually has a good selection of books on tape.

Consider reading to your boys, especially if they are not the best of readers. My wife and I used to read to our kids all the time. As they grew older, they seemed to lose interest in being read to. However, I think they really still enjoy it. I've noticed that whenever I read a passage I admire aloud to my wife, the kids always seem to show up and listen under the pretense of doing other activities. Just a few of the thousands of good books for boys are *The Red Badge of Courage*, by Stephen Crane; *Captains Courageous*, by Rudyard Kipling; *Treasure Island*, by Robert Lewis

Stevenson; *Huckleberry Finn*, by Mark Twain; *The Call of the Wild*, by Jack London; *The Hobbit*, by J. R. R. Tolkien; and *Endurance*, by Alfred Lansing. Also, the books on sports heroes published by Doubleday are great inspirational stories and easy for most to read. I've included a list of good books for boys at the end of this book. A number of websites and the local library generally have lists of good books for boys to read as well.

Before we move on, let me just interject a word of caution: as hard as it may be, try not to criticize your son's father—especially you single moms out there. Your son will learn soon enough on his own what faults his father has. You certainly don't need to praise his father, but don't constantly put him down either. I tell men I speak with, "What possible good can come from speaking ill of your children's mother—the woman they love above all else?" I think the same truth applies to their father.

On the other side of the coin, when your husband or your son's father exhibits good character traits, make sure you praise him for it. Praising him in front of your son or talking to your son about it later are very important ways to affirm positive character traits. This practice is especially effective when a husband and wife work together as a team, praising each other in front of their children. This helps children develop respect for each parent and teaches them not only how to treat each other but also how best to interact with the opposite sex. When our children were quite young, my wife, in her wisdom, began praising me in front of the children and reprimanding them when they said something disrespectful either to me or about me. I think it has made a big difference in their opinion of me as a man, father, and husband.

Conversively, if your ex-husband continually disappoints your son by missing times together or not showing up for visits, don't make excuses for him. Dr. Kevin Leman, in his book *Making Sense of the Men in Your Life*, states:

> Most divorced women already feel guilty about all their kids are going through, so they may try to cover up the ex's neglect and even cruelty, hoping to "soften" the blow. When you make excuses for your ex, your children will see through your weak explanations. They'll feel the sting of their father's unfaithfulness, and they'll have to deal with a mother's warped sense of justice. Just imagine how frightening it must be to discover you can't trust Dad or Mom![8]

When your son asks why Daddy never showed up, you have to bite back your anger and gently say, "I don't know. Why not call him and ask him?" That keeps the responsibility in the court where it belongs—with your ex-husband.[9]

If your son's father is not a good example due to alcoholism, drug addiction, philandering, irresponsibility, or any of a dozen other reasons, let your boy know he doesn't have to grow up to be like his father. In the movie *The Mighty*, the biggest fear of one of the young boys at the core of the story was that he would turn out to be a sadistic criminal like his father. He thought just because his father was a certain way, he was destined to be that way regardless of his own wishes.

No matter how it may feel sometimes, there are a lot of good men out there. They just don't get as much press coverage as the bad ones. Keep your eyes open for good men to interact with your son. Also, be aware of learning situations where you can point out examples of good male behavior. Your son needs to see what manliness looks like, and he needs to know what qualities you admire in a man.

## Questions for Discussion

1. Think about the best male role models throughout your life. Tell your son about these men and what made them important in your life.
2. Make a list of books and movies you want your son to read and see. Talk to men in your life and get recommendations of their most inspirational movies and favorite books.
3. Actively look for male mentors to be involved in your son's life. Discuss with other mothers some ways you can find these mentors.

# 10

# Where Do I Go from Here?

At this point you're probably thinking, *Okay, where do I go from here?* How do you take the information outlined in this book and create a plan to help raise up a boy to become a good man?

There's an old question, "How do you eat an elephant?" The answer: "One bite at a time." In other words, when you have a seemingly overwhelming task to perform, the best way to approach it is to get started by taking small steps. Eventually, those small steps, or bites, will add up to the entire elephant. The important thing is just to get started.

The following are small action steps you can take to implement the information in this book. I encourage you to modify these suggestions and combine them with your own ideas to develop a plan that works for you and your family.

## Recognize Your Role

Here's the good news—just the fact that you are reading this book means you are ahead of the game. It means you are aware that there are differences between males and females. It means you want to communicate with and properly discipline your son and that you want him to grow up to be a good man. Most of all, it means you care, and that's the majority of the battle. Many people are so overwhelmed by the responsibilities and stresses of everyday life that they barely have time to meet their own needs, much less those of someone else. You've chosen to spend your limited time and resources on a worthy cause—growing a boy into a good man. Good for you! You don't want to just raise your boy to chronological maturity. You want him to become a man of courage and integrity with a good work ethic and a healthy understanding of love and responsibility. The world needs men like that.

Mothers teaching their sons is part of God's plan. You have an important role in turning your boy into a man. Proverbs 1:8 urges, "My son, hear the instruction of your father, and do not forsake the law of your mother." The mother's instruction should be bound about a boy's heart and neck, a constant companion and a trusted guide.

## Pray

The most important action you can take on your son's behalf is to pray for him on a daily basis. Prayer is the most powerful tool in the universe. Pray for your son's physical, spiritual, and emotional health. Pray for God's blessings to be poured abundantly over your son. Pray that his heart will be turned toward God. Pray that he will have wisdom and discernment and that God will bring good friends into his life who will lift him up, encourage him, and hold him accountable. Pray for his sexual purity. Pray for his future spouse's sexual purity and for her parents to have godly wisdom in raising her. And pray for God to give you the wisdom to be the kind of parent he would have you be and to make you worthy of raising the child he has entrusted to your care.

Keep a prayer journal of all the things you have prayed for your son over the years. You will be stunned as you look back at just how many of those prayers God has answered.

## Plan

> Failing to plan is planning to fail.
>
> Author unknown

It has been my observation over a long period of time that goals and accomplishments don't just happen—they require planning. Think about which values and character traits you want your son to demonstrate. Then design a program to help teach him those values. Just like a large Thanksgiving dinner does not come to fruition without planning and preparation, the deliberate implementation of character traits requires some careful thought. Consider which techniques have worked best in communicating with your son and which types of disciplinary actions have been most effective. Monitor his responses and the effectiveness of different approaches you've tried and remember them for future reference.

Next, write your plan down on paper. A goal that is not written down tends to never get accomplished. Try separating your strategy into different categories. For instance, one category might be instilling certain character traits in your son. Another might be inserting positive male role models in his life. Still another will be teaching him to work, and so on.

Your plan will then need to be revisited and adjusted periodically, perhaps once a year or more. Remember that as your son grows, your responses and the way you deal with him will need to change. What works when he is seven years old will likely not work when he is seventeen.

Recently, I took an informal poll of a dozen men I respect to see what they thought were the greatest needs in a man's life. Here is a compilation of the most common answers I received. Keep these needs in mind as you consider your plan. If you want your son to grow up to be a happy and healthy man, you must find ways to start addressing these needs in his life:

1. Significance in our lives—assurance that our lives mean something. We need to know that what we are doing counts for something both now and in the future.
2. Other men in our lives—mentors, friends, and so forth. Many of the men I talk with are amazed to find that other men struggle with the same debilitating issues as they do.
3. A cause to fight for. Men are moved by great stories (e.g., films, books) but often end up more discour-

aged because they are living in the day-to-day mundaneness of life. That's why they get caught up in the fantasy of porn or sports or sex.

4. Appreciation—respect and admiration from our families and other men.

Every man has four parts to his being that need to be nurtured and developed in order for him to be fulfilled—spiritual, educational, occupational, and relational. These portions of a man's psyche have been called different things by many different people. For instance, Stu Weber tweaks them slightly and calls them the king, mentor, warrior, and friend components—the four pillars of a man's heart. All four need to be in balance for a man to fulfill his role in life.

A man needs to develop his spiritual side through a relationship with God. I've discovered we can never be happy without that relationship no matter how much we accomplish or what we achieve. A man also needs to continue to learn and develop his mind—to educate himself about life and people. A man who continues to learn continues to grow. Next, he needs to work and fulfill his responsibility as a provider and protector for his family. And lastly, he needs a loving relationship with his family, a strong marriage bond with his wife, and good friends to encourage him and hold him accountable.

As you develop your plan for your son, help him understand the components of his personality that need to be developed in order for him to be content. As you develop this plan, ask for his input and commitment to be part of the plan.

## Keep Learning

> Gold has a price, but learning is priceless.
>
> Chinese proverb

Since you've gotten this far in this book, you now know quite a bit about what makes boys tick. Don't stop now. Keep reading books and looking for positive male examples for your son. I've included a resource list at the end of this book to help you learn more about the male gender.

You'll find that you are somewhat sensitized to this subject now, and you will start noticing examples of positive and negative male behavior that you may have previously ignored. Point out these examples to your son as they occur. Have some fun with it! Have him look for poor character traits that men act out in books and movies. Keep a list of both the positive and negative characteristics men exhibit, and then make one composite man with all the negative traits and another with all the positive and see what they look like. By making your son cognizant of these traits, you are teaching him to be consciously aware of their importance.

Also, help him understand that most men exhibit both good and bad characteristics. Point out to him that we are all human and fail from time to time, but by God's grace we are forgiven and made new again.

## Involve Male Role Models

A boy who has never had healthy masculinity modeled for him faces an extremely difficult, if not impossible, task in becoming a good man. Since healthy masculinity is rarely modeled in the movies, on television, or in our cultural heroes, he will never understand how to think, act, and behave like a man without the presence of a real man in his life. Short of God's grace actively and directly intervening in his life, your son will need to find positive male role models in order to help him understand and fulfill his destiny as a man. The earlier in life he encounters these role models, the easier the road will be to travel. If his father is not available to provide a model of healthy masculinity, you *must* find role models for him. Besides prayer, this should be the number one action point of your plan.

God, who sent his Son, Jesus, to earth as a man, is the ultimate role model of masculinity. Part of your plan should include schooling your son in the teachings of Jesus Christ and the Bible so that he may develop his spiritual faith and acquire wisdom.

## Develop a Vision for Your Son

Develop a vision for your son. Always hold him to the higher standard. Yes, the narrow path is harder to walk down, and most people take the easy path through life. But easy is not always best. Your son needs to have a vision of what a man should be (hopefully, modeled by his father). He needs high standards to strive toward and goals and dreams to motivate him. Make sure you share that vision with him.

Make sure your son understands that critics are everywhere in life but that critics shouldn't stop him from doing what he wants. Teach him not to be discouraged by others' pessimism. Teach your boy not to let others stop him from achieving his dreams and goals.

## Modify Existing Programs to Fit Your Situation

In all likelihood, you are already taking a number of great steps in training your son to become a good man. I want to encourage you to keep those actions that are working for you and add whatever nuggets you've gleaned from the pages of this book. Modify programs that seem good but maybe just aren't quite working smoothly. Be aware of what other parents are successfully doing and use their strategies whenever appropriate.

Refer back to this book occasionally to pick up things that you missed or that weren't applicable at your first reading. Make this book your own: write in the margins, highlight passages for future reference, and dog-ear the pages you like. Use this book as a tool over the years as you raise your son to be a man.

## Have Fun!

One last thing I'd like you to remember: boys are fun to raise! If you understand the differences between males and females, you will enjoy raising your son beyond measure. Just remember—expect boys to be a little louder and more physically active than girls. Try not to be too overprotective of them, and keep your sense of humor. I promise, you will find no greater satisfaction in life than raising your son from a helpless baby and then seeing him exhibit strength of character beyond your wildest expectations as he enters manhood.

Let me conclude this book by giving you some encouragement. God loves you, and he loves your son. God has wonderful things in store for your son. He purposely chose you, out of all the women in the world, to be your son's mother. God knew the struggles and challenges you would face. He knew all your faults and failures as a mother, and yet he still chose you as the right person to raise his child—because he also knew all your strengths and skills. Truly, you are worthy to be your son's mother, an awesome woman.

So spend time with your son. Let him know that you love him so much that you would be willing to die for him—in the same way that Christ died for all of us. Love like that covers a multitude of mistakes.

Finally, actively seek out God's will for your son. Help him become the man of destiny God designed him to be before time began. Good parenting, and God bless you.

# Resources

## Books for Moms

Arterburn, Stephen, and Fred Stoeker. *Every Man's Battle*. Colorado Springs: WaterBrook, 2000. (To understand a man's struggle with sexual sin.)

Bassoff, Evelyn. *Between Mothers and Sons: The Making of Vital and Loving Men*. New York: Penguin, 1994.

Dobson, James. *Bringing Up Boys*. Wheaton: Tyndale, 2001.

Eldredge, John. *Wild at Heart*. Nashville: Thomas Nelson, 2001. (To understand a man's heart.)

Gurian, Michael. *A Fine Young Man*. New York: Tarcher/Putnam, 1998.

———. *The Wonder of Boys*. New York: Tarcher/Putnam, 1997.

Hoff Sommers, Christina. *The War Against Boys: How Misguided Feminism Is Harming Our Young Men*. New York: Simon & Schuster, 2000.

Leman, Kevin. *Making Sense of the Men in Your Life*. Nashville: Thomas Nelson, 2000.

Oliver, Gary and Carrie. *Raising Sons and Loving It!* Grand Rapids: Zondervan, 2000.

Weber, Stu. *Tender Warrior: God's Intention for a Man*. Sisters, OR: Multnomah, 1993. (To understand what a man should be.)

## Books for Boys

Consider reading these aloud with your boys if you can.

*The Call of the Wild,* by Jack London

*Endurance,* by Alfred Lansing

*The Hobbit,* by J. R. R. Tolkien

*Huckleberry Finn,* by Mark Twain

*Tarzan,* by Edgar Rice Burroughs

*Treasure Island,* by Robert Lewis Stevenson

Any books published before 1965 about sports heroes, pioneers, frontiersmen, soldiers, and our founding fathers usually provide good role models for boys.

## Movies for Boys

Review these first to make sure they're appropriate for your son at his current stage of development.

*Angus,* starring Kathy Bates

*Braveheart,* starring Mel Gibson

*Chariots of Fire*, starring Ben Cross
*The Emperor's Club*, starring Kevin Kline
*Gladiator*, starring Russell Crowe
*Glory*, starring Matthew Broderick
*The Green Mile*, starring Tom Hanks (Warning: graphic language and prison situations)
*Hoosiers*, starring Gene Hackman
*The Jack Bull*, starring John Cusack
*The Last of the Mohicans*, starring Daniel Day-Lewis
*The Last Samurai*, starring Tom Cruise
*Lonesome Dove*, starring Robert Duvall
*The Mighty*, starring Kieran Culkin
*The Mission*, starring Robert DeNiro
*Old Yeller*, starring Fess Parker
*Open Range*, starring Robert Duvall and Kevin Costner
*The Patriot*, starring Mel Gibson
*Pay It Forward*, starring Haley Joel Osment
*The Princess Bride*, starring Cary Elwes
*Remember the Titans*, starring Denzel Washington
*The Rookie*, starring Dennis Quaid
*Rudy*, starring Sean Astin
*Scent of a Woman*, starring Al Pacino
*Schindler's List*, starring Liam Neeson (Warning: graphic violence)
*Secondhand Lions*, starring Robert Duvall
*Signs*, starring Mel Gibson
*Simon Birch*, starring Ashley Judd
*To Kill a Mockingbird*, starring Gregory Peck

*We Were Soldiers,* starring Mel Gibson

*White Squall,* starring Jeff Bridges

Any of the Lord of the Rings, Star Wars, or Indiana Jones series

# Notes

### Chapter 1: Your Place in God's Plan for Your Son

1. Steven Pressfield, *Gates of Fire* (New York: Bantam Book, 1998), 426–27.

2. John Eldredge, *Wild at Heart* (Nashville: Thomas Nelson, 2001).

3. Ibid., 43.

4. Ibid., 53.

5. Ibid.

### Chapter 2: Why Are Boys *So* Different?

1. Gary and Carrie Oliver, *Raising Sons and Loving It!* (Grand Rapids: Zondervan, 2000), 54.

2. Michael Gurian, *A Fine Young Man* (New York: Tarcher/Putnam, 1998), 120.

3. Oliver, *Raising Sons and Loving It!*, 66.

4. Dr. James Dobson, *Bringing Up Boys* (Wheaton: Tyndale, 2001), 25–26.

5. Oliver, *Raising Sons and Loving It!*, 55.

6. Robert May, *The Case for Sex Differences: Sex and Fantasy—Patterns of Male and Female Development* (New York: Norton, 1980).

7. Dobson, *Bringing Up Boys*, 33–34.

8. Oliver, *Raising Sons and Loving It!*, 20.

9. Christina Hoff Sommers, *The War Against Boys* (New York: Simon & Schuster, 2000), 95.

10. Ibid.

11. Ibid.

12. Eldredge, *Wild at Heart*, 80.

13. Hoff Sommers, *The War Against Boys*, 1.

14. Ibid., 14.

15. Betsy Hammond, "2004 Academic Achievers Valedictorians Reverse Gender Gap," *Oregonian*, June 3, 2004.

16. Hoff Sommers, *The War Against Boys*, 14.

17. Ibid., 63.

18. Robert Lewis, *Raising a Modern Day Knight* (Wheaton: Tyndale, 1997), 65–66, originally reported on *CBS Evening News*, February 9, 1987.

19. Oliver, *Raising Sons and Loving It!*, 35.

20. Ibid, 32.

21. Ibid., 37.

## Chapter 3: Pitfalls—What to Avoid

1. Robert Lewis, *A Journey into Authentic Manhood*, tape series, sessions 6 and 7, "The Overly Bonded with Mother Wound," Fellowship Bible Church, 1997.

2. Ibid.

3. Eldredge, *Wild at Heart*, 13.

4. Lewis, *A Journey into Authentic Manhood.*

5. Eldredge, *Wild at Heart*, 35.

6. Louise J. Kaplan, *Oneness and Separateness: From Infant to Individual* (New York: Simon & Schuster, 1978), http://www.bartleby.com/66/64/32064.html.

7. Lewis, *A Journey into Authentic Manhood.*

8. Ibid.

9. Andrew Klavan, *Man and Wife* (New York: Tom Doherty, 2001), 131–33. Used by permission.

10. Lewis, *A Journey into Authentic Manhood.*

11. Robert Bly, *Iron John* (New York: Vintage Press, 1990), 2–3.

12. Lewis, *A Journey into Authentic Manhood.*

13. Eveyln Bassoff, Ph.D., *Between Mothers and Sons: The Making of Vital and Loving Men* (New York: Penguin Books, 1994), 17.

14. Eldredge, *Wild at Heart*, 11.

## Chapter 4: Boys and Sex

1. Stephen Arterburn, Fred Stoeker, with Mike Yorkey, *Every Man's Battle* (Colorado Springs: WaterBrook, 2000), 63.

2. Leman, *Making Sense of the Men in Your Life* (Nashville: Thomas Nelson, 2000), 6–7.

3. Ibid., 130.

4. Gurian, *A Fine Young Man*, 32.

5. Dr. Kevin Leman, *What a Difference a Daddy Makes* (Nashville: Thomas Nelson, 2000), 42.

6. Ibid., 44.

7. Kristen Zolten, M.A., and Nicholas Long, Ph.D., "Talking to Children about Sex," Center for Effective Parenting, 1997, http://www.parenting-ed.org/handout3/General%20Parenting%20Information/sex.htm.

8. Leman, *Making Sense of the Men in Your Life*, 44.

9. Dr. James Dobson, *Preparing for Adolescence*, tape series (Ventura, CA: Regal, 1990).

10. Dennis and Barbara Rainey, *Moments Together for Couples* (Ventura, CA: Gospel Light, 1995). Used with permission.

### Chapter 5: Communicating with Boys

1. John Gray, Ph.D., *Men Are from Mars, Women Are from Venus* (New York: HarperCollins, 1992).

2. Ibid., 16.

3. Ibid., 16–17.

4. Ibid., 37.

5. Frank Pittman, *Man Enough* (New York: G.P. Putnam's Sons, 1993), 230.

6. John Gray, Ph.D., *What Your Mother Couldn't Tell You and Your Father Didn't Know* (New York: HarperCollins, 1994), 73.

7. Gurian, *A Fine Young Man*, 237.

8. Oliver, *Raising Boys and Loving It!*, 160.

### Chapter 6: Disciplining Boys

1. Rainey, *Moments Together for Couples*. Used with permission.

2. Kelly B. Cartwright, Ph.D., "Effective Behavior Management Part IV: Consequences of Children's Behavior—Punishment," http://www.selfhelpmagazine.com/articles/child_behavior/behavman4.html.

3. Oliver, *Raising Sons and Loving It!*, 137.

4. Mary Kay Blakely, *American Mom* (Chapel Hill: Algonquin Books, 1994), prologue.

5. Oliver, *Raising Boys and Loving It!*, 139.

6. Joseph Conrad, *Heart of Darkness* (Mineola, NY: Dover, 1990). Originally published in 1899.

7. "Life Skills for Kids," www.MrsABC.com, newsletter archive.

### Chapter 7: What Do Boys Need to Learn to Become Good Men?

1. Walter Schirra Sr., quoted in *Newsweek*, February 3, 1963.

2. Calvin Coolidge, "Quoteland," http://www.quoteland.com/author.asp?AUTHOR_ID=220.

3. This story inspired the Fellowship of the Red Bandanna, a ministry of Man in the Mirror Ministries in cooperation with a number of other men's ministries, and is found on their website, www.maninthemirror.com.

4. Preston Gillham, *Things Only Men Know* (Eugene, OR: Harvest House, 1999).

## Chapter 8: Respect

1. Stephanie Martson, *The Magic of Encouragement* (New York: W. Morrow, 1990), http://www.bartleby.com/66/50/38050.html.

2. Dobson, *Bringing Up Boys*, 230.

## Chapter 9: The Importance of Male Role Models

1. Eldredge, *Wild at Heart*, 62.

2. Bassoff, *Between Mothers and Sons*, 16.

3. Eldredge, *Wild at Heart*, 62.

4. Bly, *Iron John*, 16.

5. Gurian, *A Fine Young Man*, 55.

6. Pittman, *Man Enough*, 16.

7. Ken R. Canfield, *The 7 Secrets of Effective Fathers* (Wheaton: Tyndale, 1992), 4.

8. Leman, *Making Sense of the Men in Your Life*, 221.

9. Ibid., 220.

Author and speaker **Rick Johnson** founded Better Dads, a fathering skills program, based on the urgent need to empower men to lead and serve in their families and communities. Rick's books have expanded his ministry to include influencing the whole family, with life-changing insights for men and women on parenting, marriage, and personal growth. He is a sought-after speaker at many large conferences across the US and Canada and is a popular keynote speaker at men's and women's retreats and conferences on parenting and marriage. Additionally, he is a nationally recognized expert in several areas, including the effects of fatherlessness, having been asked to deliver papers at various venues.

To find out more about Rick Johnson, his books, and the Better Dads ministry, or to schedule workshops, seminars, or speaking engagements, please visit www.betterdads.net.

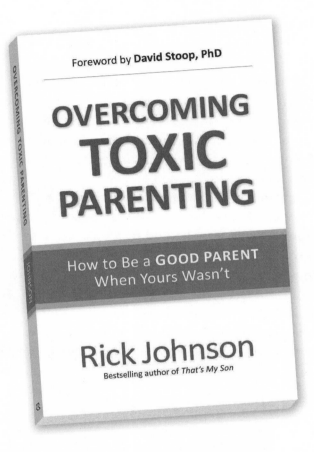